Proud Pharisees and Sadducees

Sarah More

i

COPYRIGHT

ISBN-13:978-1484087138
ISBN-10:1484087135

DEDICATION

I am dedicating this book to my beloved daughter, Eunice Malath.

CONTENTS

ACKNOWLEDGMENTS

I thank God, my daughter, Eunice Malath, parents, brothers, sisters, cousins, uncles, aunts, relatives, and friends for their patience. They allowed me to study the Bible as much as I wanted.

The following translations were used: Amplified Bible (AMP), 1899 Douay-Rheims Bible (DRB), English Standard Version (ESV), Good News Bible (GNB), Good Word (GW), International Standard Version (ISV), American Standard Version (ASV), 1965 Bible in Basic English, Contemporary English Version (CEV). Where it was not indicated, that means that is King James Version (KJV).

1 CHAPTER

THE PHARISEES

1. The origin of the name of Pharisee

Some people maintained that the name originated from an Aramaic word called "peras". They said that it was the word which was written by the hand of God on the wall of a Babylonian palace when He rebuked Belshazzar for desecrating the sacred vessels of the temple. "Then was the part of the hand sent from him; and this writing was written. And this is the writing that was written, MENE, MENE, TEKEL, UPHARSIN" (Daniel 5:24, 25, KJV).

Some people suggested that the name Pharisee originated from a Hebrew word called "Farisai'oß." It means to "set apart." It is derived from persahin, which originally was derived the word "parash." It means "to separate." Therefore, the name "Pharisee" would mean the Separatists, the Separated Ones or the Deviants.

Other people think that the name "Pharisee" is derived from the Hebrew word "parosim" which means "specifier". A Pharisee was a person who specified the correct and true meaning of the scriptures. The Greek translation is 'Pharisaios.'

The Pharisees were a very powerful religious sect during the time of Jesus and during His disciples' lifetime. "But there rose up certain of the sect of the Pharisees which believed, saying, That it was needful to circumcise them, and to command them to keep the law of Moses" (Acts 15:5, KJV).

The Pharisees sect grew out of the Maccabean soldiers known as the Hasidims, Chasidim or the pious ones. They fought against Hellenization of the faith and practices of Judaism.

Flavius Josephus, the Jewish historian, described the Pharisees as follows:

> Now, for the Pharisees, they live meanly, and despise delicacies in diet; and they follow the conduct of reason; and what that prescribes to them as good for them they do; and they think they ought earnestly to strive to observe reason's dictates for practice. They also pay a respect to such as are in years; nor are they so bold as to contradict them in anything which they have introduced; and when they determine that all things are done by fate, they do not take away the freedom from men of acting as they think fit; since their notion is, that it hath pleased God to make a temperament, whereby what he wills is done, but so that the will of man can act virtuously or viciously. They also believe that souls have an immortal rigor in them, and that under the earth there will be rewards or punishments, according as they have lived virtuously or viciously in this life; and the latter are to be detained in an everlasting prison, but that the former shall have power to revive and live again; on account of which doctrines they are able greatly to persuade the body of the people; and whatsoever they do about Divine worship, prayers, and sacrifices, they perform them according to their direction; insomuch that the cities give great attestations to them on account of their entire virtuous conduct, both in the actions of their lives and their discourses also. Flavius Josephus, Antiquities of the Jews – Book XVIII, From the Banishment of Archelaus to the Departure of the Jews from Babylon, # 1.
> http://www.ccel.org/j/josephus/works/ant-18.htm

The Pharisees taught certain methods in how to discipline the flesh in order to have self-control over everything. One of them methods was to always eat bland diet. People should not use spices, sweeteners, etc. in their foods and drinks. That way, they would gain self-control over other sins.

John the Baptist was stricter in his diet and clothing than the Pharisees who prided themselves as holy people were. They love fined clothes and dining on meats and wine. They felt bad that they were not living as strictly as John the Baptist. So they insulted him as some devil-possessed man who did not want to enjoy life. "For John came neither eating nor drinking, and they say, He hath a devil" (Matthew 11:18).

Most of the invitations given to the Messiah to eat dinners in the houses of friends were given by the Pharisees. They fed Him and His disciples well. But because He was very popular with the people and they competed in inviting Him into their houses, they insulted Him as a glutton and drunkard. "The Son of man came eating and drinking, and they say, Behold a man gluttonous, and a winebibber, a friend of publicans and sinners. But wisdom is justified of her children" (Matthew 11:19).

But actions speak louder than words. The Messiah's life was pure and sinless. He was not a gluttonous man or drunkard. He was wise, intelligent, and sober all the time.

The Pharisees love to debate the teachings of the Bible. They often encourage people of different views to oppose each other so that they could learn the pros and cons of their laws. They would follow their laws very strictly. They tried to discipline their thoughts to obey the laws.

They respect older people and would not argue with them. They believe in fatalism. They believe that good and bad things are ordained by God. People should try to receive the bad things without complaining because God wanted them to suffer. But nations or individual can always strive for their social and political freedoms.

They taught that good people would be rewarded. They would be taken to heaven but sinners would be punished in hell. They taught people how to worship God and offer sacrifices to Him.

They advocated that places of worship should not only be in Jerusalem. They should be built within walking distance for the people. People could go to Jerusalem on major feast days such as the Passover, Day of Atonement, Feast of the Trumpets, etc.

2. The Pharisees fought Sadducees common people to be ordained as priests

There was used to be only one center of learning. It was in the temple in Jerusalem. The people of Israel were scattered all over the country. They could not travel to the temple every day to learn about the Word of God.

So over the years the people started slipping back into godlessness that had made them fall as preys to the Chaldean forces led by their brilliant Commander called Nebuchadnezzar. They were their slaves for seventy years.

The Sadducees or the upper class Jews were absorbing Greek culture and pagan religion as advanced knowledge. The house of Aaron said that they were the only people in the world to be priests according to the Scriptures. "And thou shalt gird them with girdles, Aaron and his sons, and put the bonnets on them: and the priest's office shall be theirs for a perpetual statute: and thou shalt consecrate Aaron and his sons" (Exodus 29:9).

The sons of Aaron, the chief priests of the Party of the Sadducees, quoted such scriptures. They said the priesthood was their exclusive rights from God. They were the only ones to be scribes and teachers of the Law. But they mingled the teachings of the Bible with Hellenistic philosophies, logic, etc. They were despising their own culture and God as backward and inferior.

The Jews ordered that the Pharisees should teach them in the temple. They also should be the ones to offer their sacrifices because they do not call on false gods to bless them. It gave a foothold for the Pharisees to enter into the temple. But most of them were only junior priests.

As the products of the Maccabean revolutionists who fought for the Torah and Jewish culture, the Pharisees fought for the rights of the Jewish people and Gentile converts to read the Bible for themselves. They said that every Jewish man was a priest.

They quoted these scriptures: "And Moses went up unto God, and the LORD called unto him out of the mountain, saying, Thus shalt thou say to the house of Jacob, and tell the children of Israel; Ye have seen what I did unto the Egyptians, and how I bare you on eagles' wings, and brought you unto myself" (Exodus 19:3, 4).

God sent messages to all Israel and the whole world through Moses, "This is what you are to say to My house that is called Jacob. Preach the Gospel to the small and weak people of the earth. Though they are weak sinners, they are the stars of God the Elohim. You have all witnessed how I was as sharp as sword against people who stood against us.

I put you into My womb. I was pregnant with you, once again, in order to keep you safe from all harm. I walked away with you. I was like a pregnant woman carrying you in My womb and escaping with her baby safe in her womb from dangers. I have done this throughout your lives.

I carried you in My arms like an eagle carrying its young on its wings. I arrived together with you to live apart from the rest of the world and to live only in Me and so that I can shower you with My unconditional love and miracles.

He called them with endearing words and ordained all of them as His works. "Now therefore, if ye will obey my voice indeed, and keep my covenant, then ye shall be a peculiar treasure unto me above all people: for all the earth is mine: And ye shall be unto me a kingdom of priests, and an holy nation. These are the words which thou shalt speak unto the children of Israel" (Exodus 19:5, 6).

He said, "If you will listen to the Law of love coming out of My mouth, and keep and guard it in your hearts as your greatest treasure on earth, you will be to Me a covenant people. We will be a family sworn with blood to be eternally one. You will be the rarest and most expensive treasure to Me.

You will be as sweet and special as truth to Me as I am the Truth to you. Among all these swarming sinners on earth such as the demons, both you and I will be the Truth. The earth is mine. She will not continue in sin forever. She will be the truth.

As men and women of truth, you are to officiate before Me as priests and to pray and bring others to Me. Heaven and the saints are now the kingdom of righteous and holy Persons. The meanings of all these things are these: I have made you the righteous and holy ones."

The Pharisees declared that God had ordained all Jewish men to be priests before He appointed the household of Aaron to run. And so His first ordination superseded the one of Aaron.

They claimed that all the blessings of the priesthood belong to all the men of the Twelve Tribes of Israel and not only to the family of Aaron, the Levite. "The secret things belong unto the LORD our God: but those things which are revealed belong unto us and to our children forever, that we may do all the words of this law" (Deuteronomy 29:29).

The Pharisees said that the only secret things about the blessings of the priesthood and other blessings are still with God. They belong to Him but any other blessings that have been revealed in the Bible belong to everyone on earth now and forever.

The family of Aaron did not have exclusive rights to any blessing coming from the throne of the Almighty. God wants the people of the earth to receive all His spiritual blessings such as ordinations into the priesthood or workers in order to help them know His Law better and obey them more perfectly. And of course, now Christians should also know the deep meaning of the Cross of Calvary better every day.

Working for God will get their minds more involved with the Law and the Cross. It will spur them on their way to heaven. In any case, everyone should try to learn to read so that they can read the Bible for themselves. All the blessings written in the Bible belong to each one of the sons and daughters God birthed on the earth.

The Pharisees argued that all the people of Israel were to take full possessions of whatever blessings God had poured down on the earth, which of course, included being priests, scribes, and teachers of the Bible. "When Moses commanded us a law, as a possession for the assembly of Jacob" (Deuteronomy 33:4).

The Pharisees declared that all tribes of Israel are Moses himself. They were purified and made holy by the mercy of God. They were to live and preach the Law and Mosaic laws to the world exactly as Moses did.

The Law and the priesthood were given to everyone. They are like sweet aromatic perfumes. Everyone was to sniff the aroma and enjoy them. The Law and working for God would bring everyone great joy and peace.

And to help the people learn the Bible, synagogues and schools should be built for the laity anywhere in the world. If anyone of them wanted to become a priest, he was free to do so. Bible knowledge would make them live righteously and preach much more effectively than mingle truths with heretics through pride and/ignorance.

They encouraged Jews to learn reading and to participate as rabbis in their synagogues. The Sadducees were opposed to the idea because it would reduce their powers over the people. Students tend to follow their teachers. They wanted the house of Aaron to be the only priests and teachers in the land to make it easier for them to control the minds of the people.

But the Sadducees fought the Pharisees very fiercely. They did not want powers to be taken away from them. However, the general Jewish populace loved the Pharisees for standing up for them. They all knew that the priesthood had degenerated.

The high priesthood was achieved through the recommendations of Greeks and, later, Italians through briberies. If the briberies did not want, they would murder the high priest and take over his office.

The laity gave full support to the Pharisees to help them know the Bible and also become priests. Thus, encouraged, Pharisees went ahead in building numerous and Torah schools in spite of all the oppositions and persecutions they faced daily from the Sadducees. Priests and rabbis multiplied. And now thousands of Gentile converts are also priests and other workers for God.

The Jews and Christians still build schools and seminaries for teaching the truths of the Bible. They add other academics such as sciences, arts, technology, etc. to the curriculum to help their students survive in this competitive world.

The ordinary Jewish men or women knew the Bible better than the Sadducees though they prided themselves as learned in the language and cultures of the Greeks. The Jewish

7

commoners supported the Pharisees in their endeavors to see that their children were taught about God as written in the Bible, the recitation of the basic creed of Judaism or Shema, teachings of the oral laws, etc.

The laymen who were of course the Pharisees took up the challenge of teaching all Jews the Scriptures, oral laws, etc. They were hugely popular with the common people. Some of them were promoted into chief priests because the people wanted them to conduct the day-today prayers in the temple. But the position of the high priests and most chief priests remained in the hands of the

Unfortunately, the Jewish priests and teachers of the Law were afraid that the people might break the Ten Commandments again and bring the wrath of God over them. So they created many laws to protect the Ten Commandments. It is like taking all the furniture, utensils, equipment, etc. out of the house and putting in the street.

They were spending all their days in the street. They were busy learning street laws but not the moral code of the home of God. They were not entering in the Presence of God to learn love, forgiveness, joy, peace, etc.

As the years went by, more and more laws were added. They came to be known as the traditional or the fathers or the oral laws. They were called oral laws because God did not write them down on the two tablets of stone. They were manufactured by men. They had no scriptural proofs.

The lawyers were those who were well versed in the scriptures and they were sometimes called the scribes or soferim. (singular: sofer). The Torah and other Holy Writings is the Old Testament. It is called the Written Law. The oral laws used to be passed from mouth to mouth. That was why it was called the oral law. But around A.D. 100, they began to be written down in what is called the Mishna or Second law and forms a part of the Talmud.

The fault of the Pharisees did not lie in saying that all Jewish men were priests but in multiplying laws that replaced the Law of God to a very great extent. God warns in no uncertain terms, "For verily I say unto you, Till heaven and earth pass, one jot or one tittle shall in no wise pass from the law, till all be fulfilled.

Whosoever therefore shall break one of these least commandments, and shall teach men so, he shall be called the least in the kingdom of heaven: but whosoever shall do and teach them, the same shall be called great in the kingdom of heaven" (Matthew 5:18, 19).

He is saying that He is the Truth. He knows what He is talking about. He said that it will be easier for quakes to seize heaven and earth and crumble them into nothingness than for the Law to quake, break, and crumble into pieces.

Not even the little jots, dots, iotas, tittles, commas, periods, etc. will be seized with intense heat, quake or shake, and fall off from the Law that was written by the finger of God on the two tablets of stones. You are prohibited from hammering or cutting away any Law that is written in the Ten Commandments.

They will bring change and fulfillment in your life. Anyone who belittles one of Ten Commandments as unimportant to his life or her life and teachers others to break it will be called insignificant in the Kingdom of God.

He or she will be completely nothing because they have chosen disobedience to the Law. But he or she who obeys all the Ten Commandments and teaches others to obey them will be called greater than greatness itself in the Kingdom of God.

3. Priesthood is a matter of the heart and not formalities

The priests used to have ceremonial washing of the hands and feet before they offered animal sacrifices in the temple. They washed the utensils and other equipment in the temple in preparation of offering new sacrifices.

The Pharisees came up with the idea that since all Jewish men were priests they also need to perform these ceremonial washing every day. They need to wash their hands, feet, cups, plates, etc. like the priests were doing in the temple.

They went as far as saying that if they went to the market and especially touched the Gentiles, they had sinned. Their main intentions of not touching the Gentiles were to prevent them from being led into idolatries, intermarriages, etc. To keep the minds of Jews away from being attracted to the Gentiles, they taught them to look at all Non-Jews as hopeless sinners and untouchables. But washing were only for the priests to be practiced during offering of sacrifices.

The washing God wanted all of them and the Gentiles to do wash to come to Him to be washed of their sins. They were to demonstrate repentance by offering of animal and bird sacrifices in the temple.

The ceremonial washing made them feel good and clean. It made them proud and self-assured about their salvation. Unfortunately, their hearts were as sinful as of those of weak Jews and the Gentiles they despised as beyond the salvation of God. "And he called the multitude, and said unto them, Hear, and understand: Not that which goeth into the mouth defileth a man; but that which cometh out of the mouth, this defileth a man" (Matthew 15:10, 11).

The Messiah told them that since the history of the world began; eating natural foods and drinking fresh clean water have never changed the righteous into sinners. It is the thoughts that make people sinners.

They accused the Messiah of breaking their man-made

laws. "Then came to Jesus scribes and Pharisees, which were of Jerusalem, saying, Why do thy disciples transgress the tradition of the elders? for they wash not their hands when they eat bread" (Matthew 15:1, 2).

The Messiah and His disciples always washed their hands before they ate food. They took baths and kept themselves clean. The Pharisees were not accusing them of lack of hygiene but to wash their hands, feet, etc. before they ate meals just like the priests did according to the Torah before they offer sacrifices in the temple.

What comes out of the heart can make a person sin. He said, "Do not ye yet understand, that whatsoever entereth in at the mouth goeth into the belly, and is cast out into the draught? But those things which proceed out of the mouth come forth from the heart; and they defile the man.

For out of the heart proceed evil thoughts, murders, adulteries, fornications, thefts, false witness, blasphemies: These are the things which defile a man: but to eat with unwashen hands defileth not a man" (Matthew 15:17–20).

He said that the Pharisees were worried about eating of food, digestion, absorption and elimination processes. Food does not change people into demoniacs. Though they are important and one should be careful what one eats and drinks, the weightier matters are what are in your heart. Sin can change the great people of the earth who were created to be wise, intelligent, and holy into demons.

Whatever comes out of the mouth comes from the heart. And if the heart is filled with sin, sorceries or words of Satan comes out of the mouth. They are what make a person an evil person or sorcerer. Evil people who are called sorcerers in some Middle Eastern translations are adulterers, fornicators, thieves, planters of lies, blasphemers, etc.

These are the sins that make persons made in the image of God to be demoniacs. But acting like the high priest or a holy person does not change the heart. The Holy Spirit is the only one who can make a person holy.

The Messiah said that emptiness, sorrow, and sadness will follow legalists all the days of their lives unless. They are full of the things of the world. They want to own the whole world through dubious means. But they will not get the things they need the most.

It is Him, the Messiah, who they really need. "Woe unto you, scribes and Pharisees, hypocrites! for ye make clean the outside of the cup and of the platter, but within they are full of extortion and excess. Thou blind Pharisee, cleanse first that which is within the cup and platter, that the outside of them may be clean also" (Matthew 23:25, 26).

The Lord gave specific instructions of how the priests should offer sacrifices in the temple. The Jews were copying them. But they were not offering animal and bird sacrifices. They are just faking them. What good would it do for them? They are not the priests who were officiating in the temple.

All legalists and hypocrites are the same. Many people are trying to look and/or sound like the Messiah, Aaron, Moses, etc. but it will do them no good. The Messiah predicted the spiritual conditions of the majority of His professed followers in these last days as very deplorable and disgusting. "This know also, that in the last days perilous times shall come.

For men shall be lovers of their own selves, covetous, boasters, proud, blasphemers, disobedient to parents, unthankful, unholy, Without natural affection, trucebreakers, false accusers, incontinent, fierce, despisers of those that are good, Traitors, heady, highminded, lovers of pleasures more than lovers of God; Having a form of godliness, but denying the power thereof: from such turn away" (2 Timothy 3:1–5).

People are wondering, "What is going on? Why are bad things chasing us from place to place? Where can we hide from trouble?"

They are in trouble because human hearts have changed for the worse. The most dangerous people in this world are not the Muslims, Hindus, Buddhists, and other pagans. They are not the animals, birds, fishes, earthquakes, volcanoes, floods, drought, etc. but hypocrites and legalists among Christians.

They worship their own spirits. They love wealth, riches, comfort, etc. They love to elevate themselves as the greatest and the best of all peoples. They have faith in no one else but in themselves.

They are proud and arrogant. They think that they are Moses the lawgiver. Think that they are the law. They are always right. They are great people.

They curse the Name of God. They throw the glory of God under their feet. They try to elevate themselves into His place. They have refused to change their bad behaviors towards those who gave them birth and to God their Creator. But they make the lives of their parents and that of their Savior very sad.

They have stopped being thankful to their benefactors. They do not want to be persons made in the image of God. They do not want to be made whole and perfect in their thoughts, words, and actions.

They are unaffectionate, unsympathetic, without compassion, etc. They do not want to comfort people who are suffering by gathering them in their arms and speaking softly and gently to them.

They are not peacemakers but troublemakers. After people have taken time to make peace with them, they will break them and plunged everyone into wars and conflicts. "Beware of false prophets, which come to you in sheep's clothing, but inwardly they are ravening wolves" (Matthew 7:15).

Outwardly they look as holy as pious as the ancient prophets of the Lord but inwardly they are ready to jump on your like foxes on sheep and eat you alive. Like some wild animals that pretend to be a part of the livestock grazing out in the open pasture in order to eat them, hypocrites befriend good Christians in order to destroy their reputation.

They release immoralities like uncontrollable diarrhea or gallbladders that are diseased and ineffective in holding water. They are too proud to admit any of their sins. Their evilness has made them very fierce and dangerous people. They are command breakers and, therefore, demoniacs.

They have turned away from the love of those who are sweet like honey. They do not want to be good and excellent. They do not want His glory to be a part of their lives. They do not want to be like the Most High.

Instead, they pursue cruelty as a mode of life. They betray each other for a dime. They are arrogant in their thoughts and would not accept rebukes and/or discipline because of their errors. They have no love and faith in others but in themselves. They do not care for anyone except for themselves. They only pray for opportunities and/or provisions to enjoy themselves.

They are full of love for themselves, and there is no room in their hearts for love for God. Instead of coming back to Him in tears and repentance and asking Him to remove pride and selfishness from their hearts, they are running farther and farther away from Him.

They all have the pictures of perfect holiness. They look and sound like God. But they do not want to receive His power inside their souls. They treat Him and His glorious salvation for their souls like filth that are destined for the dumpsters and burning into total extinction in hell.

But you must let these hypocrites you are a good Christian. Do not make anyone of them a part of your world where you are thinking, talking, moving, and living.

Hypocrites and legalists are not hopeless cases. The Messiah suffered and died for sinners such as them. If they surrender their hearts to God, He will change their hearts. They will be like Him.

He invites them, "Behold, I stand at the door, and knock: if any man hear my voice, and open the door, I will come in to him, and will sup with him, and he with me. To him that overcometh will I grant to sit with me in my throne, even as I also overcame, and am set down with my Father in his throne" (Revelation 3:20, 21).

He is saying, "Here I am. I am standing here at your door. I will not move. I am knocking your door with My hand so long and so hard it is hurting as if set on fire. If only someone inside you can hear My voice and opens wide the door, I will enter in your heart as your Creator and Redeeming God.

We will always eat supper with you. And you will eat it with Me. I promise you very truthfully and with no doubts about it. It is a fact. Everyone who overthrows sin, I will make him to sit with Me on My own throne just as I also had overcome the world and am now sitting together with My Daddy on His throne." Listening to the voice God and following the Written Word will bring be real sanctification in your heart.

4. Faith saves but being Jewish doesn't

The Pharisees and their followers took great pride in
trying to keep their laws right. In the process, they lost sight of
God. When He told them exactly who they were in their
hearts, they were shaken. He called the people of His
hometown of Nazareth hypocrites.

They had identity crisis and blamed Him for waking up
their dead consciences. "And he said unto them, Ye will surely
say unto me this proverb, Physician, heal thyself: whatsoever
we have heard done in Capernaum, do also here in thy
country." (Luke 4:23).

He said, "You are all telling to Me saying, 'We are your
blood. As such, we have a right to tell you this proverb: as a
Physician, you are as wise a serpent. Heal yourself of all your
diseases and sicknesses. We heard that you have healed the
people in Capernaum. Perform the same miracles in your own
land of Nazareth.' You are saying that when I am healing you
of all your diseases, handicaps, resurrecting the dead, etc. I am
healing Myself."

He pointed out certain truths that they needed to know.
"And he said, Verily I say unto you, No prophet is accepted in
his own country" (Luke 4:24).

He said, "The truth that I am telling is that we are yet to
hear that a prophet has been welcomed with open arms in his
own land."

He went on to point out, "But I tell you of a truth, many
widows were in Israel in the days of Elias, when the heaven
was shut up three years and six months, when great famine
was throughout all the land; But unto none of them was Elias
sent, save unto Sarepta, a city of Sidon, unto a woman that
was a widow" (Luke 4:25, 26).

He said, "There were many widows who were living in
sorrow and abject poverty in Israel during the drought that
lasted for three and half years. Their eyes were always filled
with tears because they had no husbands to struggle to find

some food for them and their children during the long period of starvation. But the Lord God did not send Prophet Elijah to anyone of your widows here in Israel.

They were still considering themselves holy, righteous, sufficient and, therefore, in no need of God. He was sent to a widowed Gentile woman who had sorrows to the full. She was a true mourner. Her eyes were full of tears for greater things that are found only in God alone.

She had discovered the secret of sharing the little she had with other people. She was ready to be the helper of God by feeding Elijah."

He gave an example of the infectious disease of leprosy. "And many lepers were in Israel in the time of Eliseus the prophet; and none of them was cleansed, saving Naaman the Syrian" (Luke 4:27).

He said, "They were many people whose bodies were eaten with leprosy in the days of Prophet Elisha in this land of Israel. But none of their bodies were scrubbed and washed with the healing of God. Only Naaman the Syrian belonged to the Lord. He was healed of his leprosy."

When the Messiah told them that they were not Jews but a bunch of hypocrites, they were very angry. Anger made them think they were righteous men and women. They claimed they were filled with fits of holy anger for the glory of the Lord. They felt insulted.

How could the Messiah say that the only thing they cared for was how to keep the traditions of the fathers perfectly and not the Law of God? They claimed that they were not hypocrites. They were all sure and very confident of their salvation before the Lord. How could the Messiah say that the Gentiles were holier than the children of God?

They rose up as one man. They gnashed their teeth at Him like mad men and women. They rushed at him with outstretched arms. They had only one thought in their minds. It was murder. Spiritual arrogance was driving them to kill Someone in the house of prayer. They were breaking the Law they prided themselves of keeping very perfectly. "You shall not commit murder" (Exodus 20:13, AMP).

They all laid their hands on Him wanting to tear Him a part. But they decided to do give Him the most painful death.

His bones would be broken by jagged rocks. They carried Him through the narrow street, out of the gate of their town, and to the highest pick of the hill.

As they tried to push Him down the hill to break Him in a thousand pieces, He disappeared from their hands into thin air. God the Father saved Him from their murderous intentions. He promoted Him into the state of invisibility. They could not see Him.

He walked right back and among them. He made His way through the crowds. They could feel but could not see or touch Him. He walked away. He escaped from the hands of the murderers. "And all they in the synagogue, when they heard these things, were filled with wrath, And rose up, and thrust him out of the city, and led him unto the brow of the hill whereon their city was built, that they might cast him down headlong. But he passing through the midst of them went his way, And came down to Capernaum, a city of Galilee, and taught them on the Sabbath days." (Luke 4:28–31).

But the people of Capernaum saluted as their Lord and Messiah. They welcomed Him into their midst with joy. They asked Him to forget about Nazareth and what they did to Him. They asked Him to make their city his hometown.

They invited Him into their synagogues. He taught them on the Sabbath days. He healed them of all the diseases, injuries, handicaps, etc.

5. Corban

The Messiah accused them of being the enemies of the Law of God because they were giving birth to falsehoods. "But he answered and said unto them, Why do ye also transgress the commandment of God by your tradition? For God commanded, saying, Honour thy father and mother: and,

He that curseth father or mother, let him die the death. But ye say, Whosoever shall say to his father or his mother, It is a gift, by whatsoever thou mightest be profited by me; And honour not his father or his mother, he shall be free. Thus have ye made the commandment of God of none effect by your tradition" (Matthew 15:3–6).

The God of all commanded that they must honor and have mercy on their fathers and mothers. Any child who curses or insults his or her parents must be put to death. But if anyone of them told his father or mother, "Corban!"

The parents would receive no benefits from the child when he had placed the word 'Corban' on the gift. You do not need to take care of your parents when they cannot take care of themselves due to poverty, illnesses, old age, etc. God is more important than them.

When you die, all your properties will belong to the temple. The priests were enriching themselves through trickeries. The temple belonged to God and all His children. It was not the property of the priests. They had no right to enrich themselves on the expense of God.

Corban acted like a country that is walled in and without permits of entrance except for the people who live in her. The parents had no access to the help of their children because they were all hedged in by the oral laws or traditions of the fathers. When the children die, the gift which might be land, gold, jewels, houses, etc. would be taken over by the priests. The Pharisees overthrew the Law of God by their oral laws.

6.   Charity

The Savior counseled His followers that they must always strive to reach the highest standard of holiness that the Lord God their Father has set before them. They must never do anything that is less than holy. Giving help to people in need is the same like God creating things for the good of His children.

You are made to be a helper just like your Creator though He helps in magnificent, countless, and myriad ways. He does not show off when He is creating or saving people. You must learn to be humble like Him when you are giving a helping hand.

Try to avoid listening to your pride. Do not pay tithes, give offerings, and help people in need to be seen and praised by people. You must know by now that most of the people who are praising you today will curse you tomorrow.

Do not depend on people to give you the highs to help push you forward. They have the power to push you up, and they also have the power to bring you down.

If you are helping out so that people can watch you and admire you, you have all lost your rewards of golden palaces and farms that your Father who lives in the heaven above all heavens has for you. "Take heed that ye do not your alms before men, to be seen of them: otherwise ye have no reward of your Father which is in heaven" (Matthew 6:1).

When you are giving your tithes and offerings, do not make musicians to go before you blowing loud trumpet sounds to announce to everyone that you are about to give your gifts. Do not open your treasure boxes and show to the people what you are about to give to the Lord. They must never see what you are about to offer.

It is a secret just between you and your God. "Therefore when thou doest thine alms, do not sound a trumpet before thee, as the hypocrites do in the synagogues and in the streets, that they may have glory of men. Verily I say unto you, They have their reward" (Matthew 6:2).

Do the same thing when you are helping the poor, sick,

etc. in the street. Do not send musicians ahead of you to announce your arrival. They must not blow loud trumpets to draw the attention of the people that you are about to make donations for people in need.

The hypocrites do such things so that they may be admired by people. They want to be admired as very generous, pious, and awesome people. When they announce themselves by musical instruments or mouths of people that they are giving offerings, they will surely receive the admiration they are looking for. Large gifts are impressive.

It is the truth is that people will admire them for their generosity. That is the only reward they will get. There will get no reward from heaven. "But when thou doest alms, let not thy left hand know what thy right hand doeth" (Matthew 6:3).

You are blessing the name of the Lord when you give a helping hand to people in need. Do not allow people who are standing on your right hand know what you are doing for needy people. And also do not allow people who are standing on your left hand know about the works you doing for the poor, sick, etc. on behalf of the Lord.

You are giving your help out of the deep reverence and awe you have for your God. "That thine alms may be in secret: and thy Father which seeth in secret himself shall reward thee openly" (Matthew 6:4).

You Father in heaven will respect the deep reverence bordering on fear that you have for Him that made you reach out to disadvantaged people. While you did your social work without making noise about it, He will come openly for all to see when He comes to bless you.

He will bring you closer to Himself than ever before. Your life will change completely. Things will always look up for you.

7. God gave scathing rebukes to the hypocrites, legalists, and agnostics

Hypocrites are fooling themselves. They always take one forward step towards the Lord and two steps back into sin. They are mean brothers and sisters who are boxing the Lord all the time. They open their mouths to praise Him but they do not mean it. They are cursing Him instead.

They are praying that He made die with all His demands for righteousness. "And they come unto thee as the people cometh, and they sit before thee as my people, and they hear thy words, but they will not do them: for with their mouth they shew much love, but their heart goeth after their covetousness" (Ezekiel 33:31).

God gave scathing rebukes to the hypocrites, legalists, and agnostics. The professed to be the followers of the Messiah always come before Him to pray. But they treat the occasions very lightly as if He is their fellow human beings.

Some of them are respectful people. But the respect and honor that they are giving Him are the same that they are giving to their leaders and elders. They are mocking the Great One. They sit down in front of Him as if they are sitting in front of their gather own very important persons.

They lick Him all over with their tongues to please Him in order to get something out of Him. They pretend to listen to His teachings. They pretend to have understood. They make solemn vows that they will follow Him even to death.

But they are all hypocrites. They are pretenders. They have all refused to be to be taught by Him. They have rejected Him to be their Teacher. They open wide their mouths and pretend that they are worshipping and praising Him.

In all appearances they look like the holiest saints the world has ever seen. They look like as if they have received the eternal life of God and have been recreated all anew again. But God knows them very well. They are fooling each other but they cannot fool Him.

They speak words of love. But they do not mean them. Instead, those love words break hearts instead of healing and invigorating them. They are not love words but words of murder. They are killers.

Fake love kills faster than if the words were never spoken at all. They are spending all their lives and energies in chasing that extra profit or gift. The business people love the extra profits they are making on their businesses that they did not see coming more than God.

Christians demand to be given extra love and attentions because they say that they are the fathers of the Church, families, communities, governments, etc. And so when a person gives one of them a cup of something, they want to receive two or more instead of one. And they love free stuff or things. Such dealings are worth more to them than their own Maker and Messiah.

When they are singing songs to Him individually or corporately, they pay full attention to the sounds of the instruments and their own voices. They are entertaining themselves and not their Messiah.

Then, they begin to sing with their voices. They love the loveliness of their voices. The music is directed towards their own ears and feelings. And when it is good, they enjoy themselves very thoroughly. And so God is like a piece of very lovely music. And at that moment, He is very beautiful. And they want that happy mood to continue forever. It is heaven for them. They satisfy their own ideas, feelings, and desires.

They never bother themselves to be in line with the One they are claiming to worship. "And, lo, thou art unto them as a very lovely song of one that hath a pleasant voice, and can play well on an instrument: for they hear thy words, but they do them not" (Ezekiel 33:32).

Most of them take Him to be like a good speaker or entertain. If they do not hear the kinds of sermons and/or music they like, they can abandon Him. He is but good words and music that are given to entertain them and make them happy.

He is lovely and beautiful as long as He keeps them in good mood. They want Him to sweet lullabies to them as if they are little babies. They do not want to listen to solid teachings that create them into new beings. They want to hear Him speaking in a gentle voice to lull them to sleep. They do not want to face realities.

He is the good Law. They have refused to give a chance to listen to the good Law-Giver. He is the good life that is helping them to live in this world very beautiful. But they do not take much thought about Him as the beautiful Love that never ends. They do not pay attention to whatever He says. And if they hear it, they will not obey Him.

Believers have become as sly as foxes. They never speak truth from their hearts. They have rejected to live by the truth. "Nevertheless they did flatter him with their mouth, and they lied unto him with their tongues. For their heart was not right with him, neither were they stedfast in his covenant" (Psalms 78:36, 37).

Their hearts have never been sanctified to live by His divine culture. They have refused to put faith in the covenant of love and loyalty He has made with them. He sealed the covenant of eternal friendship with them on the Cross of Calvary. He salted it with His own blood.

But how see many professed Christians are roaring very angrily at Him like wild lions! They are no different than those Israelites who fought Him in the wilderness. They hurt His feelings very mercilessly. They wounded His heart very deeply. But He is not saying a word.

You can get hurt. You can disappear into oblivion forever. He is taking your insults very humbly and quietly because He loves you.

You are deceiving yourself if you think that you are powerful. You cannot push God around. But He is very sympathetic to your frailties. That is why He is not answering you as equals or you will die. "How oft did they provoke him in the wilderness, and grieve him in the desert! Yea, they turned back and tempted God, and limited the Holy One of Israel" (Psalms 78:40, 41).

When He wins your heart and you come back to Him, you tend to always fall back into that old habit of tempting Him to hit you back. You challenge Him to no end. You throw huge rocks of quarrels, complaints, insults, etc. on Him day and night. You bound His omnipotent powers up with your unbelief and doubts. And you have to gut to call all these endless quarrels true saintliness.

But God is like a good, happy, and joyful Pharaoh or King. Even though His subjects are mean and disobedient, He is full of peace and joy within Himself. Their unhappiness of His citizens does rub off on Him. Joy wells up from the bosom of His heart and flows from everlasting to everlasting.

He is still the Pharaoh no matter what His citizens say. He is anointed with eternal powers and royalties. No one can remove them from Him. No one can dispose Him from His thrown. And because of this overflowing love and joy, He still forgives His subjects.

They need that forgiveness so that they can have the permission to live in His kingdom. He refuses to lay His hands on them and wipe them out in a moment. He just wants to help

His subjects find eternal and indestructible joy and peace. "But he, being full of compassion, forgave their iniquity, and destroyed them not: yea, many a time turned he his anger away, and did not stir up all his wrath" (Psalms 78:38).

There is nothing He can gain by hanging all of them on trees. He is already a very powerful, contented, and joyful King. When they are trying to kill him, He just walks away from them because He is All-Powerful.

He is unmoved by their anger and hatred. He has refused to punish them because He is the King. He is too dignified to break out in anger and hatred like them. They are insignificant. They are passing winds that will not return again.

They need help get grounded and firm. "For he remembered that they were but flesh; a wind that passeth away, and cometh not again" (Psalms 78:39).

He is Daddy. He is determined to school His children to help them grow up right. So He keeps on forgiving their sins. He gives them multiple second chances to make the right choices and be holy people.

He is the Omnipotent Daddy that can cut the lives of all His disobedient children in a moment. But what will He gain by snuffing out the lives of the ignorant and the foolish. Without Him, they are just dirt. "For he knoweth our frame; he remembereth that we are dust" (Psalms 103:14).

He is like Surveyor that knows the landscape very thoroughly. He knows the make-up of your inner thoughts and feelings. He is like a scout who has inspected a mountain and knows all their good and bad paths.

He knows your strong and weak points. He wants you to be all powerful in your thoughts by put His omnipotent thoughts into you. They will powerful decisions that are right and holy.

He does not reach out His hand to discipline without first recalling that you are too frail to handle holy anger against sin. The whole earth will be blown out of existence by the burning breath that comes out of His mouth.

He is telling you all your sins not to discourage you but to encourage you to repent from all your sins. Pray and say, "Create in me a clean heart, O God; and renew a right spirit within me" (Psalms 51:10).

Ask Him to make your heart that of a good brother or sister to Him. He will make it stand strong in Him. He will make it a heart that is perfectly holy and righteous like. He wants your hearts to be of true brothers or sisters that can stand forever.

He is the God of life, and He will fill your heart with eternal life. He will put the everlasting Spirit into your soul. He will recreate you and you will become a completely new, righteous, and eternal person.

He is a good God. He will save you. "God is love" (1 John 4:8).

People are turning away from Bible truths. "Without natural affection, trucebreakers, false accusers, incontinent, fierce, despisers of those that are good, Traitors, heady, highminded, lovers of pleasures more than lovers of God" (2 Timothy 3:3, 4).

They are turning to the achievements of men and women in the Bible and in their races, tribes, families and of themselves as of greater glories than of God. They have made gods out of Noah, Japheth, Shem, Ham, Abraham, Moses, David, Mary, the Twelve Disciples of Jesus, Martin Luther, John Knox, Calvin, etc. Their sermons are human-centered not God-centered.

They make up exaggerate the myths of Black Egyptians as if they are part of the Bible doctrines. They dig up Buddhism, Hinduism, sorceries, magicians, etc. that they have no business doing. In the process, they get devil-possessed and do not how to pray to throw demons from off them. Sooner or later, they get used to devil-possession and use Satanic powers to persecute and/or control their Church members.

Many Christians wonder why they do not have peace when they have prayed all their lives. They are not keeping the truth that comes from the heart of a loving God that can give them peace and joy. Instead, they love and admire each other more than their Creator. They are drunk with pride.

People are abandoning the truths that came from the Messiah's own mouth. They do not want prophecies and testimonies of the Holy Spirit about God the Father and God the Son.

Their lusts for self-exaltations have paved the way for son of sin to go around claiming that he is the Christ. He is drawing millions of people to follow him. "Let no man deceive you by any means: for that day shall not come, except there come a falling away first, and that man of sin be revealed, the son of perdition;

Who opposeth and exalteth himself above all that is called God, or that is worshipped; so that he as God sitteth in the temple of God, shewing himself that he is God" (2 Thessalonians 2:3, 4).

This is the spirit of transgressions has spread abroad. It is blinding the eyes of men and women who love flatteries, money, fame, etc. They love delusions rather the word of truth. They drink falsehoods like sweet wine.

They are intoxicated by the alcohol of legalism or demoniac teachings. They are drunk with the wisdom of the earth. They never seem to understand divine wisdom that created heaven and the earth.

When you present the pure word of God to the people, they will be attracted to Him. They will love you for pointing the way to Christ. But if you spend most of time in exalting the saints, histories, race, families, cultures, what are the fundamental beliefs of Islam, Buddhism, Hinduism, etc. you will invite competition from other preachers. They will want to talk learned and educated like you.

You will hate for trying to be like you, and they will have for having knowledge they do not have. But if they hate you for preaching spiritual facts, the Lord Himself will deal with them. They may hate or kill you but they will be answerable to your Creator what they doing to you. "If any man teach otherwise, and consent not to wholesome words, even the words of our Lord Jesus Christ, and to the doctrine which is according to godliness;

He is proud, knowing nothing, but doting about questions and strifes of words, whereof cometh envy, strife, railings, evil surmisings, Perverse disputings of men of corrupt minds, and destitute of the truth, supposing that gain is godliness: from such withdraw thyself" (1 Timothy 6:3–5).

Preach the truth. Let the Messiah deal with the frictions in the churches between preachers, Bible teachers, etc. He will speak for Him and scare your enemies to death.

If one is preaching dung, he or she does not know Christ the Messiah. He or she is going round and round in self-conceit. He or she has not learned anything about the Messiah.

As such, He or she does understand Him at all. He or she will depend or telling stories that exalt human beings, rules and laws not of heaven but of earthly governments, etc. They will trouble each other for nothing. Their works will not lead people to the Messiah.

Relationships are poisoned. Grudges and revengeful thoughts will dominate the heart. They argue over civilian duties but not the works of the soldiers of the Cross. These doctrines are not from God. Earthly doctrines make people turn each other like ferocious man-eating lions.

They devour each other like hungry lions instead of exalting the word of truth together. They are fooling themselves when they assume successes in this life means that they holy.

Since they are lions, be careful about. You do not turn your back to lions when you are very close. They can get some intimidations if you stare boldly straight into their eyes and at the same time, you are walking back.

When you far or behind some bushes, turn and run as fast as your legs can carry you. You do the same things with these

Anti-Christs. Run but make you they do not jump on you and hurt you for abandoning them and their demoniac doctrines.

It is the sacred work of all church members to see to it strange doctrines are not entertained. Especially upon the shoulders of the elders is this responsibility exacted by the Messiah. No church member is allowed to alter the truths of the Bible.

Some men and women love attention and admiration. They will even use sorceries to steal the works of other people and preach them as their own bible studies. The temptation to steal is very great among some TB evangelists.

They love making outstanding remarks so that the audience can shout: "Oh-h-h-h! Ah-h-h-h! Amen!" Etc. They love the shouting, clapping, etc. They are to kill to be famous, appear on TV, etc.

The Messiah only asks that you present the truth as it is and nothing more. He wants to be humble. It is better to be boring then to make earth-shaking remarks that you stole from someone through sorceries. Do not oppress people in order to be the only voice in the Church.

Every man, woman or child whose heart is touched by Lord has a testimony. Do not persecute or murder them if they want to witness for the Lord who died for their sins and get the full adoption rights of be the sons and daughters of God.

Do not use the pulpit to show off how you are better than other races or families in relationship to God. For example, speculations about genealogies that can prove that you are the blood relative of Jesus Christ, St. Paul, St Luke the Greek, St Paul, Cornelius the Italian, etc. in order to show to the world that you have a special place in the heart of God more the others.

He does not have favorites. If anything, people who had learnt something about Him but did not follow through with His salvation and in some cases are stills suffering more than recent converts, for example, the Jews, Arabs, Lebanese, Syrians, Iranians, Iraqis, Jordanians, Egyptians, Libyans, Sudanese, Ethiopians, Greeks, Italians, etc.

Some of them should have been the superpowers of the world. But powers went to those whose ancestors knew nothing about God the cradle of the world did not take their blessings very seriously and worked on them.

There is nothing to show off about your ancestors' relationships with the Lord. He does not love you more than other people whose ancestors are not registered in the Bible or in the history of the Christian church such as the reformations. He loves everyone equally because He made each one of them.

Preach the Law of God as it is. Do not read your own opinions and feelings into it. Do not preach or quote it to pass judgments on people. The Law points people to Christ and not away from Him. "Let us not therefore judge one another anymore: but judge this rather, that no man put a stumbling block or an occasion to fall in his brother's way." Romans 14:13).

Jesus has never appointed to head His kingdom on this earth. He is her King, Lord and Judge. He is the one to judge people whether they will have a right to live with Him or not. You have no right to ostracize or pass death sentences on people to be burned in hell.

Call the people to come and receive their blessings from the Lord. They have inheritances waiting for them in heaven. So you point out their sins in order for them to be blessed when they repent.

Do not broadcast the weakness of your brothers and sisters to the whole world. Your rude and contemptible attitude will discourage them and chasing them away from following the Lord.

8. Nicodemus

Though most of the Pharisees were hypocrites and legalists, there were some who were faithful followers of the God of heaven. When they met the Messiah, they did not have difficulties into believing that He was the Son of God. All the prophecies of the Old Testament were being fulfilled right before their eyes in the Body of the Messiah.

They were two very powerful Senators who were secret followers of the Messiah. One of them was Nicodemus. He was one of the wealthiest Jews in Jerusalem.

He had a private interview with the Messiah at night when he could have all his audience without the interruptions of his fellow Pharisees who were very jealous of Him. "There was a man of the Pharisees, named Nicodemus, a ruler of the Jews:

The same came to Jesus by night, and said unto him, Rabbi, we know that thou art a teacher come from God: for no man can do these miracles that thou doest, except God be with him" (John 3:1, 3).

The Messiah taught him several very important truths. He said that everyone needs to be born against by the spirit just as they were born by their parents. "Marvel not that I said unto thee, Ye must be born again. The wind bloweth where it listeth, and thou hearest the sound thereof, but canst not tell whence it cometh, and whither it goeth: so is every one that is born of the Spirit" (John 3:7, 8).

Though flesh is important, it is secondary to the spirit. It is the Spirit of God that is giving intelligent live in the people. And that Spirit can birth eternal life that is filled with peace, joy, unconditional love, eternity, etc. into the souls of the believers again.

The Messiah taught him about the importance of the Cross. He said that His death on the Cross is the salvation of the world. Israel had rebelled against God in the wilderness. They wanted to be left alone to do whatever they wanted. They chased God out of the camp. Satan sent poisonous snakes to be them and wipe them out. They were being beaten by these and were dying in their thousands.

When they cried to God to save them from death, He asked Moses to hang a brass serpent on a wooden cross. Any Israel who looked at the brass serpent as form of the God of salvation who can swallowed up Satan and all demons and save His children would be saved. (Numbers 21:9).

The Messiah compared Himself to that brass serpent. He said that the Cross was necessary in order to draw people out of sin and death and bring them to Him. "And as Moses lifted up the serpent in the wilderness, even so must the Son of man be lifted up: That whosoever believeth in him should not perish, but have eternal life" (John 3:14, 15).

He then told Nicodemus the heart of the Gospel. It is the love of God for a dying world. This love was demonstrated when He allowed His Son to become a Human Being, suffer and die for the sins of the world so that they may live again. He wants to save them.

He wants to give them a secured, happy, and eternal life that He Himself has. "For God so loved the world, that he gave his only begotten Son, that whosoever believeth in him should not perish, but have everlasting life" (John 3:16).

The Pharisees had sent soldiers to arrest the Messiah and kill Him. But He was so loving, winsome and His sermons were so good that they did not arrest Him. They listened very attentively to His sermons until He finished spirit.

The priests asked the soldiers very angrily as to why they had not arrested the Messiah. "The officers answered, Never man spake like this man" (John 7:46).

The Pharisees mocked the soldiers as deceived and not as wise as they and the Jewish leaders were. They would not surrender their positions to Him. They began to hatch up a plan for killing the Messiah.

After the interview, Nicodemus tried as best as possible to protect the Messiah. He used his senatorial powers to thwart any plans his fellow senators were trying to hatch up to put the Messiah to death.

He asked his fellow Senators as to the legality of condemning someone to death in absentia. "Nicodemus saith unto them, (he that came to Jesus by night, being one of them,)

Doth our law judge any man, before it hear him, and know what he doeth? They answered and said unto him, Art thou also of Galilee? Search, and look: for out of Galilee ariseth no prophet" (John 7:50–52).

Nicodemus' statement shut them up. They were murderers. They wanted to kill Someone who did nothing wrong. They would not even permit Him to defend Himself. Any further discussions about killing the Messiah would constitute murder in their hands. "And every man went unto his own house" (John 7:53).

Didn't the law of Moses said that the person must defend himself? And not only the accused could defend himself or herself but he or she could come with several witnesses to back up his or her testimony.

9. Joseph of Arimathea

Joseph of Arimathea was a fellow Senator of Nicodemus. He was also a very wealthy man. He was so wealthy that he wanted to be buried like a king. He employed people to dig a grave in the rock on the side of Mount Calvary. He planted a beautiful garden in front of the garden.

He was a secret lover of the Messiah. When the Messiah died, he came out of his hiding. He went boldly to Pilate Governor and asked to bury the body of the Messiah. Pilate liked him and Nicodemus very much because they were fabulously rich.

He wanted to be their friends. They were richer than the high priests who sold the Messiah into the hands of Rome for the sake of positions as leaders of Israel. The Governor knew they would give him and his family anything he wanted. He wanted to be their friends.

He gave them permission to bury the Messiah. "And after this Joseph of Arimathaea, being a disciple of Jesus, but secretly for fear of the Jews, besought Pilate that he might take away the body of Jesus: and Pilate gave him leave. He came therefore, and took the body of Jesus.

And there came also Nicodemus, which at the first came to Jesus by night, and brought a mixture of myrrh and aloes, about an hundred pound weight. Then took they the body of Jesus, and wound it in linen clothes with the spices, as the manner of the Jews is to bury.

Now in the place where he was crucified there was a garden; and in the garden a new sepulchre, wherein was never man yet laid. There laid they Jesus therefore because of the Jews' preparation day; for the sepulchre was nigh at hand" (John 19:38–42).

10. The conversion of many priests and Pharisees

After the death and resurrection of the Messiah, many priests and Pharisees got converted into Christianity. "And the word of God increased; and the number of the disciples multiplied in Jerusalem greatly; and a great company of the priests were obedient to the faith" (Acts 6:7).

The word of God draws people closer to Him in love. Every day, He is drawing you closer and closer to Himself because His nature and character is love. He is giving births to new children every day. They had been sinners. But now He is birthing His Spirit into them and making them new people.

They are all His beloved disciples. They will serve Him eternally. They will more potent, powerful, and magnificent than bulls. They are the men and women of faith.

The temple was burnt down by the Romans in 70 A.D. Many Jews were slaughtered. Some of them were sold into slavery. Others escaped in different parts of the world.

The politico-religious powers of the Pharisees came to an end. But their teachings still persist in Judaism, Christianity, and Islam. They were the fathers of these three world religions.

2 CHAPTER

A PHARISEE AND A PUBLICAN WENT TO PRAY

He pitied the Pharisees in pretending to be holy men and women. They were acting like a group of little children who wanted to entertain another group of children by singing wedding or funeral songs but the others refused to have fun with them. "But whereunto shall I liken this generation? It is like unto children sitting in the markets, and calling unto their fellows, And saying, We have piped unto you, and ye have not danced; we have mourned unto you, and ye have not lamented" (Matthew 11:16, 17).

There are people who are trusting in their own strength to be like God. They covered themselves with clothes of self-righteousness. They live for themselves. They consider themselves as mature spiritual men and women who need no tutoring in the way of holiness.

They look down on everybody else as hopeless sinners. They put themselves first in everything and treat people who do not belong to their religious groups as the last of all peoples. These are the people with the mentality of the Pharisees.

They are eaten up by spiritual arrogance. "And he spake this parable unto certain which trusted in themselves that they were righteous, and despised others: Two men went up into the temple to pray; the one a Pharisee, and the other a publican" (Luke 18:9, 10).

There are two groups of people in the church. One group is the spiritually arrogant people. The other group knows that they are sinners. Among them are backsliders who have been living lives of street people. That is why they are called publicans. They are concerned about the affairs of this world. They are not going about doing the King's business like all good soldiers of the Cross should do. But they are contrite about their sins.

Worship is an admission of the truthfulness of God. He is loving, merciful, kind, forgiving, joyous, peaceful, etc. The worshipper admits that God is excellent in everything. He does not keep His awesome life for Himself alone.

Some of His excellent characteristics and powers will rub off on the worshipper. And the worshipper will also become great and awesome, too. The worshipper wants the most excellent life which is found in the God he or she worships.

The life of God is not only great and excellent but sweeter than honey. It is awesome, restful like the Sabbath day, and very sweet. But in order to get this excellent life, every worshipper must crucify his or her pride. Unfortunately, hypocrites and legalists like the proud Pharisees have not understood the true meaning of worship.

Instead of praying to God, hypocrites and legalists pray to themselves as if they are God. They take great pride in fulfilling every requirement of the Law. They are the proud Pharisees. "The Pharisee stood and prayed thus with himself, God, I thank thee, that I am not as other men are, extortioners, unjust, adulterers, or even as this publican" (Matthew 18:11).

The prayers of legalists are basically the same. Like the Pharisee, each of them tend to pray, "God who always desires me and is with me, I am thanking you that I am not yet like other men (and women) who have reduced themselves and others into nothing because of their sins.

They cut the chances of other people in order to make livelihoods for themselves. They steal, swindle and extort the vulnerable and naïve in order to enrich themselves on their expenses. They are thieves and robbers.

Men and women of this world do not play by fair games. They are crooks and unrighteous. They are unfair to others in order to get by. They do not have faith in You like I do. They are completely immoral.

I have seen them committing adulteries with My own eyes. But I am holy and righteous and not like one of them. In fact, one of them is standing right beside here in the church. He is from the streets. He has no knowledge of the Ten Commandments and the significant of the Cross of Calvary. "I

fast twice in the week, I give tithes of all that I possess"
(Matthew 18:12). I fast more often than these weak Christians
do. I pay my tithe even of the little herbs you have given me to
eat."

The definition of the word public means the community.
It may also mean something that is done for the common good
of the community, state or country. But it can be used for to
class people such as prostitutes as people who are free for all.
Thieves see other people's gold, jewels, money, etc. as public
properties.

The poor residential quarters in some Middle Easter cities
where poverty, crimes, prostitution, thieves, illiteracy,
godlessness, etc. are common are given names that are
variations of the name the publicans. The stigma of calling
people that are deemed to be unspiritual has not died out.

As usual, the publicans or street people stand at the back
of the church. Hostile eyes are directed towards them. They
feel their sins down deep in their souls. They are
uncomfortable and ashamed of themselves. They have abused
themselves with immoralities, alcoholic beverages, drugs,
stealing, robberies, murders, curses, Sabbath-breakings, lies,
etc. They are dirty sinners.

Unfortunately, they are also fearful of God. They do not
sure that He loves them. He has already forgiven them all their
terrible sins.

One of these unspiritual guys had the boldness to enter
the temple. But he had no right to take front seat among the
spiritualized civilized spiritual leaders of the people. His sins
were written all over his face.

They were well known by the community. He did not
have the courage to look into the disdainful eyes of the
Pharisees and Sadducees. He could not raise his eyes towards
heaven.

He felt very unworthy of the love and forgiveness of God.
"And the publican, standing afar off, would not lift up so
much as his eyes unto heaven, but smote upon his breast,
saying, God be merciful to me a sinner" (Luke 18:13).

His sorrow was so deep that that it hurt his chest very
terribly. Tears flowed down his face and beards. He hit his
chest with his fist mourning. He cried, "God who is with me!

Have mercy upon me! I have cut off myself from You. I have given you everything that is evil."

The Messiah approved him as a better spiritual man than the legalistic and proud Pharisee. "I tell you, this man went down to his house justified rather than the other: for every one that exalteth himself shall be abased; and he that humbleth himself shall be exalted" (Luke 18:14).

He said that when the man descended down from the temple and went to his house, he was a saint. All his sins were forgiven. He was no longer a publican or a man who lives in streets by jungle laws.

He had changed. His sins were washed away. He was a respected and dearly loved child of God. He was a grown and mature spiritual man like was Abraham when he offered up Isaac as a sacrificial gift of love to God.

But the sins of the Pharisee were not forgiven. And so will be the sins of hypocrites and legalists. They will not be forgiven because the proud worshippers feel no remorse for them. They are legalistic, pride, and narrow-minded.

Everyone who exalts his or her spirit above the holy and Supernatural Spirit God will be brought down. But everyone who demotes his or her spirit before the Lord as someone who is a sinner and needs love and forgiveness will be exalted as the friend of God.

2. Invite the Messiah into your heart

God's whole body was broken with punches, lashes, slaps, etc. Divine blood flowed. Crown of thorns were sunk into His skull. Divine blood flowed. He was nailed to the cross with His hands and feet. Divine blood flowed. His heart was pierced with a spear even when He was already dead.

Divine blood and water flowed. God's blood flowed all over the world. It found you. If encircled you. It waited for you to invite Him into your heart. Hopefully, you have already invited Christ into your soul.

Please stop being a hypocrite like that Pharisee who condemned a poor sinner to the Lord in the church. If you have not yet accepted Jesus Christ as your personal Savior, He is kindly, gently and lovingly asking you to welcome Him into your heart right now. He wants to save you.

You heard His voice. It is full of love, concern for your safety, kindness and gentleness. As your Loving Shepherd, He says, "But he that entereth in by the door is the shepherd of the sheep. To him the porter openeth: and the sheep hear his voice. And he calleth his own sheep by name and leadeth them out. And when he hath let out his own sheep, he goeth before them: and the sheep follow him, because they know his voice" (John 10:2–4, DRB).

You invited your Christ into your heart. You asked Him to take over the control of your mind, heart, body and spirit. But He found that you were dead inside. Your spirit was dead. Sin killed you.

Your heart was filled with hatred against God, false gods, immorality, murderous thoughts, thieving, disobedience to parents, pride, hate, envy, greed, lies, etc. Your heart was filled with sin. It was very dirty and muddied with sin. Sin was as red as foul-smelling deadly blood in your soul.

Dr. Jesus started treating you with the medicine of His own life. He began resurrection your spiritual life back from the dead. He nurses you every day by giving you His strength. He tells you what to do and what not to do.

God's divine life-giving blood began to transfuse itself

into your soul through washing away your sins. He sucked away your sins and killed them. He transfused Himself into your soul.

He washed your heart clean just as He had promised. "Come now, and let us reason together, saith the LORD: though your sins be as scarlet, they shall be as white as snow; though they be red like crimson, they shall be as wool" (Isaiah 1:18).

Have you observed the hard voices coming from pagans? They may sound gentle but there is hardness in their voices. Their voices are lifeless and so are their feelings and spirit. They are dead. You were once like them. You were spiritually dead inside. But now the Holy Spirit is softening your hard feelings and voice.

He is waking up your dead spirit. He is putting Himself into you so that you may have a new sinless spirit just like His. To crown it all, Jesus is coming back soon to take you home to your Father in heaven.

If you have already invited Him into your soul, He has just started the work of sanctification in your life. You are far from being perfect like your heavenly Father. You are lukewarm. He wants to make you into a boiling pot of hot water brimming over with love for God to drink. He does not enjoy drinking warm water.

Indeed, no one enjoys drinking lukewarm water. People enjoy drinking hot or cold refreshing water. He is kindly and lovingly counseling you to come into His saving arms. "And to the angel (messenger) of the assembly (church) in Laodicea write: These are the words of the Amen, the trusty and faithful and true Witness, the Origin and Beginning and Author of God's creation: [Isaiah 55:4; Proverbs 8:22.]

I know your [record of] works and what you are doing; you are neither cold nor hot. Would that you were cold or hot! So, because you are lukewarm and neither cold nor hot, will I spew you out of my mouth! For you say, I am rich; I have prospered and grown wealthy, and I am in need of nothing; and you do not realize and understand that you are wretched, pitiable, poor, blind, and naked. [Hosea 12:8.]

Therefore I counsel you to purchase from Me gold refined and tested by fire, that you may be [truly] wealthy, and white clothes to clothe you and to keep the shame of your nudity from being seen, and salve to put on your eyes, that you may see.

Those whom I [dearly and tenderly] love, I tell their faults and convict and convince and reprove and chasten [I discipline and instruct them]. So be enthusiastic and in earnest and burning with zeal and repent [changing your mind and attitude]. [Prov. 3:12.]" (Revelation 2:14–19, AMP).

Ask Jesus to come into your heart. He is inviting you to let Him in. "Behold, I stand at the door and knock; if anyone hears and listens to and heeds My voice and opens the door, I will come in to him and will eat with him, and he [will eat] with Me.

He who overcomes (is victorious), I will grant him to sit beside Me on My throne, as I Myself overcame (was victorious) and sat down beside My Father on His throne. He who is able to hear, let him listen to and heed what the [Holy] Spirit says to the assemblies (churches)" (Revelation 3:20–22, AMP). He will make you to live again just like He is giving life to the holy angels day by day.

3 CHAPTER

THE SADDUCEES

I. The Sadducees were agnostics

The Sadducees were from the royal and/or rich families of Israel. They were highly educated but in the Hellenistic or Greek knowledge. Greek was the lingua franca of those days. It was the language of education and distinction. But together with Greek came Greek religions and culture which were in direct opposition to the plain Word of God.

The religion was based on nature worship. The gods were created to exalt men and women. Human beings were in control even of hell and death. They were the super species over even God Himself. They were gods and goddesses.

The Greeks did not have Bible knowledge and, therefore, no personal experiences with the God of heaven like Israel. Some people among the Hamites were converts.

The first priest was a Hamite. He was called Melchizedek. He was a native or Canaanite and the King of Jerusalem. He was the priest of Abraham and Lot. Some people from other Semitic tribes also had personal encounter with God. Nebuchadnezzar the Chaldeans heard His voice.

A whole city of the Assyrians called Nineveh converted to God at the preaching of Prophet Jonah. Naaman came from Syria of the Hamitic race came to God in Israel for healing. Several Black kings, queens, and dignitaries were converts such as Jethro the priest. He was the mentor of Moses.

The Queen of Sheba was converted into Judaism by King Solomon; Rufus carried the Cross of the Messiah, etc. But the Greeks did not have close proximity with Middle East to learn of God before their invasions into Israel. So they were more to be pitied than the noble families of Judah who should have been better spiritual people than the poor Greeks who had no knowledge of the God of heaven and the earth.

The Greek system of education was built on paganism. It made the royal families of Judah agnostics or skeptics in the spiritual teachings of Judaism.

Flavius Josephus, the Jewish historian described them thus:

> **But the doctrine of the Sadducees is this: That souls die with the bodies; nor do they regard the observation of any thing besides what the law enjoins them; for they think it an instance of virtue to dispute with those teachers of philosophy whom they frequent: but this doctrine is received but by a few, yet by those still of the greatest dignity. But they are able to do almost nothing of themselves; for when they become magistrates, as they are unwillingly and by force sometimes obliged to be, they addict themselves to the notions of the Pharisees, because the multitude would not otherwise bear them. Flavius Josephus, From the Banishment of Archelaus to the Departure of the Jews from Babylon, Antiquities of the Jews – Book, # 1.**

II.   Annas and Caiaphas

James Tissot, 1896-1902, Annas & Caiaphas James Tissot

The Sadducees believe that it is impossible to prove the existence of God. They claim that if He ever existed, He had withdrawn Himself into heaven and allow the natural laws of nature to run their courses.

As such everyone should live as best as they could. You got to do what you got to do. It was no wonder that when an opportunity availed itself in the house of Annas the High Priest in form of a young virgin girl, Caiaphas took her in order to get close to her father as a son-in-law and entitled to the high priest.

And sure enough, the father-in-law recommended him to the Romans and he was appointed as the high priest. But the Bible clearly stated that a new high priest could be appointed only on the death of the reigning high priest. But Annas was very much alive.

The Jews could not abandon him just because the Romans ordered them to. So at the trial of Jesus, there were two high priests sitting as judges. They were Annas and Caiaphas.

Annas was very a powerful man in Israel. He had the ears of the Roman government. He had five of his sons besides Caiaphas appointed as high priests. The high priests with the periods of their reigns from the family of High Priest Annas who was also called Ananu or Ananias were as follows:

1. Annas ben Seth (A.D. 6–15)
2. Eleazar ben Ananus (A.D. 16–17)
3. Joseph ben Caiaphas the son-in-law (A.D. 18–36/37),
4. Jonathan ben Ananus (A.D. 36/37–44)
5. Theophilus ben Ananus (A.D. 37–41)
6. Matthias ben Ananus (A.D. 43)
7. Ananus ben Ananus (A.D. 63).

III.   The doctrines of the Sadducees

The doctrine of the Sadducees stated that there was no help for mankind from God. They had no future glory in heaven. They should use any available opportunities to help themselves.

This pagan attitude led them to friend the generally despised pagan Romans who were brutalizing their people and bribed them to place them in important offices such as of the high priest, other positions of senior priests, magistrates, tax collectors, councilors of their parliament or Sanhedrin, etc.

Enjoy the fame, riches, power, etc. of this world by all possible means. There is no future for pious and holy people. Live down here and now. Do what you can to forge yourself ahead.

The respect and loving given to the neighbors were based on them being used stepping stones to climb higher grounds of glory for one's self. The end justifies the means.

Because of the evil ways the Sadducees and leading Pharisees were treating their less fortunate fellow Jews and Gentiles, John the Baptist called brood of vipers. "But when he saw many of the Pharisees and Sadducees come to his baptism, he said unto them, O generation of vipers, who hath warned you to flee from the wrath to come?" (Matthew 3:7).

John said that they were the sons who were born by vipers and not the God of heaven. They were demoniacs. Who could teach Satan?

If they think now they need God, they needed to have true heart conversions and not have this lip service while their hearts are far from Him. "Bring forth therefore fruits meet for repentance: And think not to say within yourselves, We have Abraham to our father: for I say unto you, that God is able of these stones to raise up children unto Abraham" (Matthew 3:8, 9, KJV).

The natural sons and daughters that Sarah, Hagar, and Keturah gave to Abraham including their father himself do not have access to heaven based on the power of human blood just like the Gentiles. Everyone gets into heaven through the permission of God the Father which He has given on the Body of His Son, the Messiah of the world.

If everyone on earth rejects Him, He will make new sons and daughters that will love Him out of the rocks just like He had made all of you out of the dust of the soil.

If they do not change, they were on their way to eternal death. How? The ax of God is already at the feet to cut them down and cast them away forever. "And now also the axe is laid unto the root of the trees: therefore every tree which bringeth not forth good fruit is hewn down, and cast into the fire" (Matthew 3:10).

Politically, the Sadducees were more powerful than the Pharisees. They were the wealthiest Jews. But their demise came when Israel was overthrown by the Romans in A.D. 70.

The Sadducees believed that there is no resurrection. "For the Sadducees say that there is no resurrection, neither angel, nor spirit: but the Pharisees confess both" (Acts 23:8).

What did they mean? First, they meant to say that there is no ongoing judgment before the throne of God to decide who is a sinner and who is a saint.

Yet the Bible plainly states about an ongoing judgment at this time. "I beheld till the thrones were cast down, and the Ancient of days did sit, whose garment was white as snow, and the hair of his head like the pure wool: his throne was like the fiery flame, and his wheels as burning fire.

A fiery stream issued and came forth from before him: thousand thousands ministered unto him, and ten thousand times ten thousand stood before him: the judgment was set, and the books were opened" (Daniel 7:9, 10).

Every thought, word and action that has not been given to Jesus to deal with, is recorded against the person who committed it. The sinner will pay for the crime with his or her own life in hell. But Jesus has already died for lives that have been surrender into His hands. He has died for their sins.

Secondly, the claim the Sadducees gave in disannulling the doctrine of resurrection was because there were the mouthpiece of Satan. The judgment is good for the saints. How long will good people live with diehard sinners, demons, death, etc.? What is there reward of men and women if they decide to be decent and righteous people? God promised to take them to heaven. They would in eternal peace.

What about those who, after listening to the Gospel, persist in being demoniacs? They will suffer extermination by hell fire. This earth must be brought back to her Edenic, perfect, and holy state once again. God cannot tolerate evil this world forever.

To support their argument against the resurrection of the just, the Sadducees used the story of a woman who was married to seven brothers. This was how their argument went: "The same day came to him the Sadducees, which say that there is no resurrection, and asked him, Saying, Master, Moses said, If a man die, having no children, his brother shall marry his wife, and raise up seed unto his brother.

Now there were with us seven brethren: and the first, when he had married a wife, deceased, and, having no issue, left his wife unto his brother: Likewise the second also, and the third, unto the seventh. And last of all the woman died also. Therefore in the resurrection whose wife shall she be of the seven? for they all had her" (Matthew 22:23–28).

Whose wife will she be in heaven? Surely, heaven is a ludicrous idea. If there will ever be one, it would be a totally immoral and chaotic place.

People who remarried after their spouses had died and all of them went to heaven will share spouses. Instead of heaven being a place of peace, it will be chaotic to human existence.

God is the God of marriage, love, and social order. Heaven is the place where everyone can find that ultimate love that their souls have been longing for. "Jesus answered and said unto them, Ye do err, not knowing the scriptures, nor the power of God.

For in the resurrection they neither marry, nor are given in marriage, but are as the angels of God in heaven" (Matthew 22:29, 30). Jesus said, "You are trying to entice us to believe in your errors.

You do not know what has been written in the Scriptures. You do not even any idea about the powers of God. Had you know that He is the Omnipotent God, you will know that on the day of resurrection, He will bring the saints and recreate them into full and complete people without cravings for intimate sexual relationships. They will be fulfilled like Him.

So there is no need for marriage or come into oneness with another person in order for people completeness of the soul. They will be perfect, complete and full in everywhere.

Instead of having two Adams that were taken out of the first man, each man and woman will be a complete Adam. Adam and Eve was, actually, one person.

He was the first Adam. Each of the recreated man or woman will not have the nature that long for intimacies like the first Adam had. But they will be like the Second Adam with the endowments of supernatural love that will not crave for attention like the first Adam felt before Eve was created.

The Messiah continued to explain, "But as touching the resurrection of the dead, have ye not read that which was spoken unto you by God, saying, I am the God of Abraham, and the God of Isaac, and the God of Jacob? God is not the God of the dead, but of the living" (Matthew 22:31).

He said, "Now concerning your coming resurrection for those among who have died, you need to understand what has been written as you are reading them. They have been spoken directly to every one of you by God when He welcomed you back into His arms.

He said that He who is the God of Abraham. And He is He who is the God of Isaac. And He is He who is the God of Jacob. He is the God of each individual person on earth whether they are dead or alive. He has never been the God of dead people.

The god of death is Satan. But He who is your God is the God in whom everlasting life exists. All the saints you think are dead such as Abraham, Isaac, and Jacob are alive in the sight of God the Father of this world.

He does not look at their dust but at what they will be at the resurrection. He will look at you like that when you are resting in your dusty bad. You will live again on the day of resurrection."

One of the doctrines of the Bible is the belief in the existence of Angelology. This is the belief in the existence of holy angels. It also believes in the existence Demonology. Evil angels exist.

Since the Pharisee annulled resurrection, heaven, and hell, they said there is no hope for mankind beyond the grave. Once dead, they will remain dead. There is no resurrection for them. There is no hope of immortality for mankind. Mankind does not of God living in them.

This agnostic attitude towards God is plain unbelief. It is paganism clothed with the garment of Judaism or Christianity. In order to retain their positions as high priests, senior administrators of the priestly hierarchy, temple administrators, etc. they pretended to be spiritual men.

The Messiah condemned the teachings of the Pharisees and Sadducees in strongest possible words. "Then Jesus said unto them, Take heed and beware of the leaven of the Pharisees and of the Sadducees" (Matthew 16:6).

The teachings of the Pharisees and Sadducees were not the pure and holy teachings of God but yeast or Satanic doctrines. They were slipping into His Church like yeast working in pure lump of floor and make it to rise and taste like a decaying matter or mold.

Though the Pharisees believed in most of the spiritual contexts of the Bible, their hearts were unconverted. They loved money as much as the Sadducees did.

The Messiah warned believers not to try to give equal services to God and this world. It does not work. "No servant can serve two masters: for either he will hate the one, and love the other; or else he will hold to the one, and despise the other. Ye cannot serve God and mammon.

And the Pharisees also, who were covetous, heard all these things: and they derided him" (Luke 16:13, 14). The Pharisees and Sadducees were worshipping money as God.

The Sadducees only upheld the Torah, the Pentateuch or the Five Books of Moses. They did not recognize the rest of the Books that together with the Torah is now called the Old Testament.

They did not study the Torah to learn the spiritual context God was teaching them and the whole world. They applied the Torah literally as a Book of Law in dealing in their courts. "And if any mischief follow, then thou shalt give life for life, for eye, tooth for tooth, hand for hand, foot for foot, Burning for burning, wound for wound, stripe for stripe" (Exodus 21:23–25).

The laws of Moses were drastic laws. There was no

mercy. The people were told. "If someone does not treat you sweetly like honey, give him the same treatment. If he is not excellent in his dealings with you, give him the same treatment. If someone crucifies a person, give him the same punishment. Crucify him.

They listed the kinds of punishments to be given to offenders in a book that they called the "Book of Decrees." Queen Salome Alexandra of Judea abolished this law enacted by the Sadducees. The people of Israel were very happy with their queen. They celebrated as a holiday.

4 CHAPTER

THE PHARISEES AND SADDUCEES QUESTIONS THE MESSIAH IN ORDER TO TRAP HIM FOR EXECUTION

1. No divorces

The Pharisees gathered around the Messiah with malicious intents. They began to throw rocks of temptations at Him. They wanted Him to speak evil about marriage so that they can accuse Him before the Sanhedrin as pervert and have Him executed. "The Pharisees also came unto him, tempting him, and saying unto him, Is it lawful for a man to put away his wife for every cause?" (Matthew 19:3).

They told Him that they knew the reasons why the Law was given to men to obey. It was to make men awesome, powerful, and sweet like honey. In order to be able achieve that perfection, what should he do with disagreeable wives? In order to make himself sweet, lovely, and holy, can he divorce one who was taken out of him for any dislike, quarrel, disagreement, fight or when he does not love her anymore?

This was clearly a trap. About seventy years earlier, the Pharisees had made divorce in Israel difficult. But they pretended that things were very bad in spousal relationships. They just wanted to trap Him and accuse Him of social contempt and transgressor of God's law should He sympathize with the boys' club and order women out of marriages for any reason men wanted.

Queen Salome Alexandra (139 to 67 BC) ruled Judah for ten years from 77 to 67 BC). The Pharisees used to be a persecuted sect during the time of her husband. But she brought them out of obscurity. She appointed them to very high positions in her government and in the ecclesiastical hierarchy of the day. They were very grateful to her for helping them. They started to support the causes of women. They abolished some of the laws of Moses as discriminatory against women.

Moses laid down the law that a woman must be a virgin at the consummation of their marriage. Her parents would spread a white bed sheet on the bed. In the morning, they would show to the in-laws and especially the son-in-law that their daughter was a virgin. They would take the stained sheet home and keep it in a safe place.

When the man would try to divorce their daughter by accusing her of prostitution, the parents would bring out the stained sheet and show the town elders. "A man might marry a woman, sleep with her, and decide he doesn't like her. Then he might make up charges against her and ruin her reputation by saying, "I married this woman. But when I slept with her, I found out she wasn't a virgin."

The girl's father and mother must go to the city gate where the leaders of the city are and submit the evidence that their daughter was a virgin. The girl's father will tell the leaders, "I gave my daughter in marriage to this man, but he doesn't like her.

Now he has made up charges against her. He says he found out that my daughter wasn't a virgin. But here's the evidence!" Then the girl's parents must spread out the cloth in front of the leaders of the city." (Deuteronomy 22:13–17, GW).

They would accuse him of defamation of their family name. "The leaders of that city must take the man and punish him. They will fined him 2½ pounds of silver and give it to the girl's father. The husband ruined the reputation of an Israelite virgin. She will continue to be his wife, and he can never divorce her as long as he lives" (Deuteronomy 22:18, 19, GW).

But if the parents were too naïve and did not lay a sheet on the night of the first consummation of love of the newlyweds, the man can accuse his wife of immorality. The parents had no proof. She would lose her life.

If she was a good girl but her hyphen got ruptured accidently, and there was no proof of virginity, she would die. A man might have raped her and the case was not brought to justice. She might have been deceived by an evil man and lost her virginity.

Whatever the case, if there was no proof of virginity, she would die. "But if the charge is true, and no evidence that the girl was a virgin can be found, they must take the girl to the entrance of her father's house.

The men of her city must stone her to death because she has committed such a godless act in Israel: She had sex before marriage, while she was still living in her father's house. You must get rid of this evil" (Deuteronomy 22:20, 21, GW).

The Pharisees asked Queen Salome Alexandra to outlaw this law. They said that men should be led by modesty and decency when talking about their wives. Proofs of virginity must no more be brought before the elders whether she was a virgin or not. Women must not be put to public shame any more.

Another law of Moses declared that if a woman has the flow of blood during to child birth or menstruation, she was unclean. She might be carrying infectious diseases. She should not touch people, sit on beds, chairs, touch any utensils, etc.

She was treated like a leper. "The LORD spoke to Moses, "Tell the Israelites: When a woman gives birth to a boy, she will be unclean for seven days. This is the same number of days she is unclean for her monthly period.

Then she must stay at home for 33 days in order to be made clean from her bleeding. She must not touch anything holy or go into the holy place until the days needed to make her clean are over. "When a woman gives birth to a girl, she will be unclean as in her monthly period. However, she will be unclean for two weeks. Then she must stay at home for 66 days in order to be made clean from her bleeding" (Leviticus 12:1, 2, 4, 5, GW).

Women were excluded from carrying temple services. But the Pharisees opened the way for women to light the candles on Friday evenings before the beginning of the Sabbath day in their homes. They and their husbands were to conduct Sabbath services on Friday evenings and at the close of the Sabbath in the evenings in their homes.

The Pharisees accused some men of being greedy and capricious. They had forced the parents of the women to bring gifts and lay them on the table for eligible bachelors to be able to marry their daughters.

In the olden days, men were the ones giving gifts to the parents of the girls. But now greedy men had turned the law around. The parents of the girls were paying for the men to marry their daughters.

One of the single women lost her ten silver coins that her parents had kept in the treasure box for her upcoming marriage. When she lost one of the coins, she almost lost her mind. The Messiah reported about it. "Either what woman having ten pieces of silver, if she lose one piece, doth not light a candle, and sweep the house, and seek diligently till she find it?

And when she hath found it, she calleth her friends and her neighbours together, saying, Rejoice with me; for I have found the piece which I had lost. Likewise, I say unto you, there is joy in the presence of the angels of God over one sinner that repenteth" (Luke 15:8–10).

Some men had taken the advantage of women paying for their marriages for enriching themselves on the expenses of their wives. For example, he married and she brought ten silver coins.

After a while, he would cook up some reasons for divorcing her. Then, he would marry again; the second wife would bring him another pile of ten silver coins. He would go on divorcing and marrying to accumulate some capital for starting a business.

The Pharisees laid down strict marital laws to prevent these kinds of greedy and capricious men from divorcing their wives for gain. So when they were asking the Messiah if they could divorce their wives for any reason, they were lying. At the time in Israel, divorcing women were not as easy as it used to be before the reign of Queen Salome Alexandra.

The Messiah knew that the Pharisees were looking for ways to kill Him by asking Him to give rulings for men to divorce their wives based on whims, greed, and sheer stupidity. He put them on the spot. He gave them an awesome answer.

He directed their mind to the scriptures. Every argument must be proved right by the Word of God. "And he answered and said unto them, Have ye not read, that he which made them at the beginning made them male and female, And said, For this cause shall a man leave father and mother, and shall cleave to his wife: and they twain shall be one flesh?" (Matthew 19:4, 5).

God created men and women as His own properties. Any violence done to the weaker sex through physical or mental abusive, unlawful separations of unbiblical divorces is a sin that is committed against her Maker.

Man is the firstborn. His duty is to look after the lastborn of God. They may disagree and fight, but they are brother and sister. They are family of God. There is no divorce between a brother and his sister.

God created man as the thought and the woman as the expressions of that thought. She expresses righteousness, holiness, perfection, and unconditional love. She is the culture or tradition of the expression of righteousness.

When a man as the thought of God and the woman as the expression of that thought united in marriage, they make one whole person. That wholeness is the character and appearance of God the Creator.

The man is the remembrance of righteousness like remembering the Sabbath day to keep it holy. He is like the Sabbath day. (Exodus 20:8).

The woman is the sanctifying power that makes the Sabbath day sacred. The Sabbath day is need but it needs to be sanctified to be a holy day in order for it to be the Lord's Day. But a man and woman are needed to make unified body like the Sabbath day for them to be united in a one and holy matrimony before the Lord.

When a man and a woman unite in holy matrimony, they display the beauty and loveliness of God in way in the way the love each other and are committed. A man breaks away from the umbrella of his father's household to start a new family as sanctioned by the Lord when humans started to live on this earth.

Therefore, you must never try to deface God from this world by your divorces. He says, "Wherefore they are no more twain, but one flesh. What therefore God hath joined together, let not man put asunder" (Matthew 19:6).

Marriage is about God and his love for the world. It is not about human lusts and whims. They have no right to use what God has ordained in the Garden of Eden as access to immoralities, power, riches, fame, etc.

The blood of the men ran cold when the Creator of marriage explained why He sanctioned matrimony. It is about Him and not about men or even women for that matter. "They say unto him, Why did Moses then command to give a writing of divorcement, and to put her away?" (Matthew 19:7).

The asked the Lord that if marriage is about God and for His glory alone, then why did Moses permit discontent men to kick their wives out of their houses by just giving them divorce certificates.

He said that divorce was permitted by Moses because they would not listen to him or to God. They had very hard feelings towards him and their Creator which they demonstrated to their wives. He told them not to divorce but they would not listen. So he tried to help them to make it at least legal.

He told them not to divorce but they would not listen. So he tried to help them to make it at least legal. They had hard, unfeeling, unsympathetic, unforgiving, and unloving hearts. It is because of the cold hearted hearts that divorce was permitted. "He saith unto them, Moses because of the hardness of your hearts suffered you to put away your wives: but from the beginning it was not so.

And I say unto you, Whosoever shall put away his wife, except it be for fornication, and shall marry another, committeth adultery: and whoso marrieth her which is put away doth commit adultery" (Matthew 19:8, 9).

People who are marrying unbiblically divorced men and women are committing adulteries. Unless they repent, they will not be saved. Unlawful divorces are the transgressions of the Sixth Commandment. "Thou shalt not commit adultery" (Exodus 20:14).

Even divorce is legal that might have come about because the wife had committed adultery with someone, it is still sin. "And this have ye done again, covering the altar of the LORD with tears, with weeping, and with crying out, insomuch that he regardeth not the offering any more, or receiveth it with good will at your hand" (Malachi 2:13).

The first sin that turns the Lord away from answering the prayers of people is idolatry. Idolaters have replaced Him with Satan. So what can He do for them? The second sin that disturbs Him very much and puts Him off is the unlawful divorces.

Yet, you have never heard people that complain very terribly like people who are divorcing their spouses for no good reason at all. They are the loudest in their complaints. They go around shedding tears before God and other people that they have been wronged, and that was why they had to divorce. 'Irreconcilable differences' is the famous quotation in many a divorce case of these days.

Many of them have the courage for the failures of their marriages when they were the cause of the break-ups. Many people are baffled. They do not know what these divorce-seekers mean.

They go on to wed new brides or bridegrooms without adequate spiritual and mental preparations. Crush follow after crush leaving their lives empty and hollow. These are not the kind of lives the Lord has ordained for them. T

They must learn to sit quietly at His feet and learn love, forgiveness, patience, etc. because they tie the knots again. "Yet ye say, Wherefore? Because the LORD hath been witness between thee and the wife of thy youth, against whom thou hast dealt treacherously: yet is she thy companion, and the wife of thy covenant.

And did not he make one? Yet had he the residue of the spirit. And wherefore one? That he might seek a godly seed. Therefore take heed to your spirit, and let none deal treacherously against the wife of his youth" (Malachi 2:14, 5).

The husband and his wife are really one spirit and one body. Eve was taken out of the body of Adam. None of them has the power to separate him into two divorced persons. Even after the divorce, their spirits are still one spirit. It cannot divine itself to become two people again. The spirit is the thought or memories that each of them will carry with them to their graves.

God wants a united spirit at home just like He had made on in Adam before he was divided into two individual people so that He can have children in the form of His firstborn son.

All sons and daughters are His firstborn son called Adam. They are holy children. They are born without learned sins. And he wants the parents to live together at least for the sake of the children. He really hates divorce. It is worst on children than on the fighting spouses.

But the men seem not to get it that God hates divorce. The disciples whined about not divorcing at all. Some of them had walked away from their wives and children and were not communicating any more with them. "His disciples say unto him, If the case of the man be so with his wife, it is not good to marry" (Matthew 19:10).

God told them they were not impotent. Most of them had married. That was a sacred gift from their Creator. They should not annul their marriages.

People who are born impotent or chose that lifestyle so that they can devote their whole lives for the spread of the Gospel are above blame concerning marriage and divorces.

But once a person is married, he or she must stay married. "But he said unto them, All men cannot receive this saying, save they to whom it is given. For there are some eunuchs, which were so born from their mother's womb: and there are some eunuchs, which were made eunuchs of men: and there be eunuchs, which have made themselves eunuchs for the kingdom of heaven's sake. He that is able to receive it, let him receive it" (Matthew 19:11, 12).

And what better way can a person demonstrate the character of God when he or she refuses to divorce an unfaithful spouse. Yet, adultery does allow divorce. But there are no finer Christians than those whose love have been spurned but they decided to stay together because they love Jesus.

2. Paying taxes to Caesar

The first introduction of taxation by the Romans into Israel took place during the time of the Messiah's birth. Joseph and Mary were forced to travel from Nazareth to Bethlehem to register for the census even though she was very heavy. She was about to give birth to the Messiah.

The distance was about 140 miles by road but seventy miles as the crow flies directly. But Rome respected no pregnant mothers or people with other handicaps and ailments. People were ordered to go where the families originated from. Joseph was descendant of King David of the town of Bethlehem. He had to go there for registration and start paying taxes immediate.

A certain man by name of Judas dared to declare that taxation by foreigners was illegal. Many Jews flocked to his standard. They ran into the remote desert of Israel to raise up resistance forces that would expel the Romans from their country in the way they had overthrown the Greeks. But their enemies were too powerful for them.

They were mowed down like grass. "After this man rose up Judas of Galilee in the days of the taxing, and drew away much people after him: he also perished; and all, even as many as obeyed him, were dispersed" (Acts 5:37).

Not all the Jews came to his stand. The high priests and their friends supported the Romans. They found their offices by the permission of Rome. Good Jews could hardly stand them because they work for their own personal interests and not for the common good of their people.

Once again, the Pharisees and the Sadducees wanted to betray the Messiah into the hands of the Romans like they did with Judas. Both men were from Galilee. Judas did rebel. But the Messiah was a peaceful Man. It was true that He was the King of Israel. But He advocated peace not violence.

A hostile group of Pharisees surrounded the Messiah.

Envy and jealousies were killing them. The Messiah knew the scriptures more than any Jew born on earth. He did many miracles. He even perform the most difficult that has defeated all mankind right from Adam. That was the resurrection from the dead.

He raised Lazarus and many other dead people to life. The people loved him. Even among the united Sanhedrin members and the priesthood, they were men who were His secret followers. They planned His death that day.

They would surrender Him to the ironed will Roman Imperial Government. They would have no qualms about murdering Him if they would accuse Him of disobeying the direct orders of the Caesars about paying taxes to them. The thing they hate the most was to hear that Israel wanted to secede.

Of course, if the Messiah was reported to tell the Jews not to pay taxes, He wanted to be the King of Israel. He was the only one in existence who was born to the throne of King David, His father.

The case against Him had built. It was solid and without loop holes. He would be executed by the Romans if He was mobilizing Israel against them.

The spies from the politico-religious Party of the Pharisees and the politicians from the party of King Herod surrounded the Messiah to deal with Him. But they pretended to be spiritual men. They were the disciples of leading Pharisees and the political wing of Israel, the Herodians. But they were recruited to spy on people.

The Messiah was a threat to their government because He was born to inherent the throne of His father, King David. "Then went the Pharisees, and took counsel how they might entangle him in his talk.

And they sent out unto him their disciples with the Herodians, saying, Master, we know that thou art true, and teachest the way of God in truth, neither carest thou for any man: for thou regardest not the person of men" (Matthew 22:15, 16).

They want to hear God speaks something that was politically incorrect so that they might arrest Him and have executed. They said that they knew Him to be a Teacher who could crow like a cock His mind without fear. He was teaching the way of God that was built on truth.

His loincloth was tied loosely in readiness to wrestle any enemy who oppose Him. He was afraid of no one. He does not watch other people or listen to what they are saying in order to imitate them.

They said that since He was very brave and was not afraid of anyone, namely, the Roman Empire, the high priests and their soldiers, the high priests, and Sadducees, and the Sanhedrin, tell Him tell them the one thing everyone was afraid to make comments. Israel was under the Roman rule. Should they secede by first withholding taxes to Caesar? Tell us therefore, What thinkest thou? Is it lawful to give tribute unto Caesar, or not?" (Matthew 22:17).

They wanted to know whether Israel should continue to put shoes on Caesar's feet to help run well. Putting on shoes on his feet meant paying taxes.

The Messiah knew that the brothers were up to no good. They were spies. They wanted to implicate Him with the Caesars to have Him get killed by the Roman soldiers if should He tell them not to pay taxes.

They were the ones transgressing the Law of God as well as that of the Caesars that all the countries under their rule must pay taxes. He told them to their faces that they were not witnessing for God by calling themselves disciples of the religious Pharisees. T

They were pretenders. They were spies sent by their leaders. He asked them why they were ready to throw rocks at Him by asking Him a question that would invite a swift death on Him from their enemies, the Romans. "But Jesus perceived their wickedness, and said, Why tempt ye me, ye hypocrites? Shew me the tribute money. And they brought unto him a penny.

And he saith unto them, Whose is this image and superscription? They say unto him, Caesar's. Then saith he unto them, Render therefore unto Caesar the things which are Caesar's; and unto God the things that are God's." (Matthew 22:18–21).

He asked them to show Him what kind of wealth they were they using to put a roof over Caesar's head, clothes on his back, and shoes on his feet. He gave him a denarius. It was a local coin they were using in those days. He asked them to identify the picture of the man on the coin. They said it belonged to the Roman emperor.

He told them give the Romans their taxes, and to give God His tithes and offerings that have been laid on them for thousands of years. The money changers were in the temple courtyard that could change the Roman dinarii into temple coins for them. They should offer to God the coins of Israel had been ordered by their Jewish leaders.

The mouths of the spies dropped open with shock. He had pointed them out as spies, which was true. He revealed that they wanted to implicate with the Romans. Again, that was true. He advised them to pay respects were they were due.

They were to continue to pay taxes to the Romans because they had allowed themselves to be ruled by foreign. They were not also to forget that they were the children of God and should support His work by paying Him tithes and offerings. "When they had heard these words, they marvelled, and left him, and went their way" (Matthew 22:22).

Some of the Roman soldiers might have been around. And they would have arrested Jesus right away and put Him to death for inciting a rebellion against Imperial Rome before He could have finished His mission on earth. The spies stopped arguing with Him that day. They left Him for a while.

3. No marriage in heaven

After the Pharisees failed to trap the Messiah about paying taxes to the Romans, the Sadducees came up to test Him. The Party of the Sadducees was the part of the high priests, most senior priest, princes, lords, etc. of the Jews. They were all rich men. They were satisfied with what they had secured for themselves.

They taught demoniac doctrines. They said heaven and hell did not exist. They did not believe in good and bad angels. Heaven was here and now.

They believe that God existed. But they claimed after He had created this world, He withdrew into heaven and allowed the natural laws to run the world. So you have to do the best you can for yourself.

They, often, bribed the Romans with money to give them the office of the high priests. Sometimes, the murdered the reigning high priest in order to be promoted into his office. "For the Sadducees hold that there is no resurrection, nor angel nor spirit, but the Pharisees declare openly and speak out freely, acknowledging [their belief in] them both" (Acts 23:8, AMP).

The basic doctrines of the Christians were expounded by the Messiah and supported by the Pharisees. They believe in the existence of God who is very much involved in human affairs.

Heaven exists and the good people will be rewarded by being taken there. Unrepentant sinners will go to hell. Good and bad angels existed.

The Sadducees mixed the teachings of the Bible with Greek fables. They looked at Greek culture as more advanced than that of the Jews. To them, it was a mark of advancement to speak in Greek and behave like Hellenists.

They encouraged people to take any opportunity of advancement even if it has shady deals. Heaven is here and now and not in the sky. So you got to enjoy this world as much as you can because there was no future.

With this kind of mind set, they came to the Messiah with a question. "The same day came to him the Sadducees, which say that there is no resurrection, and asked him, Saying, Master, Moses said, If a man die, having no children, his brother shall marry his wife, and raise up seed unto his brother.

Now there were with us seven brethren: and the first, when he had married a wife, deceased, and, having no issue, left his wife unto his brother: Likewise the second also, and the third, unto the seventh. And last of all the woman died also. Therefore in the resurrection whose wife shall she be of the seven? for they all had her" (Matthew 22:23–28).

They asked, "Oh, Teacher who teaches the things of God, Moses had spoken to us on His behalf. He said, 'When a man dies when the Righteous Lord had not given him the love (children) of God, let him marry his brother's widow.

He will bring life into the world. The children will be called his brother's children. In this way, his brother's descendants will continue to exist in this world. He will be considered a potent man'

We had living amongst us seven brothers. They all loved each other very much. They obeyed the laws of Moses. The first brother married but then died. He did not yet meet with God of love who enables men to produce His righteous seed. Death brought separation between him and his wife.

Now, the second brother did what God had ordered him to do. He wedded his brother's widow. But he, too, died. Each of the seven brothers married the same woman but none of them had children with her. They all passed away one after another. Finally, the woman followed the brothers into the grave.

When the next life has started from the time when the saints will resurrection from the dead, who amongst these seven righteous brothers will she belong to as his beloved wife? They had all loved her."

It was the question that Sadducees used for mocking the Pharisees who believed that heaven exist. And the later did not know how to explain it. "Jesus answered and said unto them, Ye do err, not knowing the scriptures, nor the power of God"

(Matthew 22:29).

The Righteous Messiah told them frankly that they were deceived by god of this world in this regard. They did not know the scriptures that had been put in writing. That was why they did not the loving God. And as such, they did not know how Omnipotence and Omni-Benevolence.

He said the men of this present world come onto the women because they want their needs to be met. The women are given in marriage by their parents to the men.

They come onto them so that their needs, too, could be met by the men. "And Jesus answering said unto them, The children of this world marry, and are given in marriage" (Luke 20:34).

But God being with them, the One who counts them as excellent as Himself, will take them to heaven. He is their Daddy. They will rise up from the dead and stand powerful and strong on their own feet.

Each of them will be the Excellent and All-Loving Man or Woman just like God. They will not come onto each other to have their needs met. "But they which shall be accounted worthy to obtain that world, and the resurrection from the dead, neither marry, nor are given in marriage" (Luke 20:35).

Death will not beat them up. It will not kill them anymore. They are the love of God. They are His beloved children.

They will arise from their graves as the beloved and powerful children of resurrection. "Neither can they die any more: for they are equal unto the angels; and are the children of God, being the children of the resurrection" (Luke 20:36).

He quoted the scriptures to the Sadducees. "Now that the dead are raised, even Moses shewed at the bush, when he calleth the Lord the God of Abraham, and the God of Isaac, and the God of Jacob" (Luke 20:37).

He said, "The dead will be raised back to life. They will stand on their own feet. They will all be powerful. The omnipotent hand was on Moses at the burning bush. He commanded Moses to call Him the loving God of Abraham, the loving God of Isaac, and the loving God of Jacob."

An eternity is but a snap of the eye to Him. He sees all the dead people as if they have already risen. "For he is not a God of the dead, but of the living: for all live unto him" (Luke 20:38).

He is not the God of dead people. For then, He would be the God of death. But He is with you all. He is the God of life and love.

The dead are all alive in Him. Resurrecting them from the graves is not a big deal Him except to those who will resurrected. "And some of the scribes replied, Teacher, you have spoken well and expertly [so that there is no room for blame]. For they did not dare to question Him further " (Luke 20:39, 40, AMP).

They told Him that He explained about love and the powerful in the most excellent way possible. None of them came to Him to prove that they were more righteous like Him again. They did not ask the Righteous and Loving God any more questions.

Out desperations, the Sadducees called false witnesses in order to execute the Messiah. They asked help from the Pharisees, they were too willingly to render it. They succeeded in murdering Him. But He came back from the grave as God the Eternal. His enemies are all dead.

5 CHAPTER

PAUL THE PHARISEE

1. Saul the murderer

Most Israelis at the time of Jesus and Paul were Pharisees although the general populace was less observant of their traditional or oral law than the strict than their religious leaders of the Pharisaic and Essenes sects. The other notable sect was the Sadducees. The former sect was composed mostly of senior priests and the nobilities. The latter were Ultra Orthodox.

They were stricter in keeping the Law than the strictest Pharisees. They lived kind of a monastic but communal kind of life away from the beehive of human activities that were generally careless and godless.

The Pharisees were strict-law keepers and acted as policemen on the Jewish race and proselytes or pagan who converted to Judaism. Anyone found breaking the law was sent to court and judge by fines and, sometimes, death.

They were worried that Jews might not be keeping the Ten Commandments right. Their intentions were good but they ended up creating too many frivolous laws to help the people not to break the Ten Commandments.

They were called oral laws or the tradition of the fathers. These man-made laws made the lives of Jews very difficult and joyless. Even the Pharisees found them unpalatable. They created ways in circumventing their own laws while ordering all others to keep them.

They were unspiritual laws and, therefore, not spiritually uplifting. They were a lot of dissatisfactions among the Jews about the traditional laws. They longed for the pure and simple explanations of the Torah, Psalms, histories and poets concerning their God and the Messiah. Jesus asked the Pharisees to stop ordering the people to obey oral laws which they themselves found difficult to follow.

On several occasions the Lord challenged on the validity of their laws. In one of them, the Pharisees complained that the disciples were not washing their hands before they ate. This was not the regular washing of hands to remove dirt and germs from the hands before one would eat but a ceremonial hand washing.

They believed that if backslidden Jews such as tax collectors, prostitutes, etc. touched them, their garments and/or bodies would carry some of their sins with them. It was worse when they were touched by unconverted Gentile pagans.

They would be covered with sins. So they had to perform ritual washing of the hands and, sometimes, feet before they would partake of any meal. "But he answered and said unto them, Why do ye also transgress the commandment of God by your tradition? For God commanded, saying, Honour thy father and mother: and, He that curseth father or mother, let him die the death.

But ye say, Whosoever shall say to his father or his mother, It is a gift, by whatsoever thou mightest be profited by me; And honour not his father or his mother, he shall be free. Thus have ye made the commandment of God of none effect by your tradition" (Matthew 15:3-6).

Jesus told them hygienic washing was enough. There is no need to do ritual washing because their hearts were clean and pure before the Lord if they were following Him. Being touched by a backslidden Jews and pagans would not transfer the sins of those sinners into their minds and hearts and defiling them.

Do not force yourself and other people to follow a set of beliefs that did not originate from your Creator. He is also your Savior, Jesus Christ, your Lord. God's Law is excellent. You cannot make additions or subtractions from it. It will make you an excellent mind and heart if you follow them faithful.

The Law is not your enemy. It is your friend. It is telling you that you are a sinner and in need of a Savior. When you come to Jesus, He will wash away your sins and help you to keep the Law right. He will make you a morally and spiritually strong person.

The way you think, talk and live is not of the highest standard. You are fallible. Even if you are holy and sinless, you cannot create holiness, righteous, eternal life, etc. in other people.

The Creator is their only Redeemer. Teach them no heresies or bad theologies. You are not their Savior no matter how intelligent, wise and holy you are.

The Lord has ordered you to fulfill all the Ten Commandments for His glory and the well-being of your neighbors. Start loving and caring for your neighbors beginning, first of all, with your own parents just as the Bible has instructed you.

Whether they are good or bad is not the issue: the issue is: are you loving them for the sake of Christ and giving them all the help they need that you are able to give? That is what Jesus is looking for from you. Your parents are also ordered to love and care for their parents and so on.

Everyone is a slave of God and of the whole world. No one is born to live for himself or herself. Love is divine slavery to someone either to God and/or to other people.

It is good for the soul and invigorates the spirit to excel in doing good works. If you have no love, you will shrivel and die inside. You will become a mechanical man or woman without tender and virtuous passions, affections and love.

The Ten Commandments are non-negotiable. You do them or you will go to hell. Whenever you fail in obeying anyone or all of them, pray to Jesus and ask for forgiveness and start again obeying the Ten Commandments again.

The worst hypocrisy is when Judeo-Christians break some parts or all of the Commandments claiming that they are doing so for the glory of their Creator. He has this to say about such kinds of people. "This people draweth nigh unto me with their mouth, and honoureth me with their lips; but their heart is far from me. But in vain they do worship me, teaching for doctrines the commandments of men" (Matthew 15:8, 9).

The show-offs have mouths but no hearts. They can say glory words and pretend to live glory lives but their false religious interpretations are taking them farther and farther away from their Savior.

These are men and women made in the form of God in

physically appearance and use of brain powers. There is no excuse for any to divert from the Law of God.

He has given you enough brain power to do that which is right. Stop worshipping the Lord in bad own ways. It is bad. Do not teach others to worship Him by following your erroneous ways. It is murder. If they get lost, you will be responsible for their eternal deaths.

Not all Pharisees were bad people. They did a lot of good in Israel and the whole wide world. The Pharisees knew the Ten Commandments by heart but not their spiritual context.

When some of them like Paul and the Twelve Disciples met Jesus and were converted into following not just the written Ten Commandments but their spiritual contexts, the blood of the Lamb, faith, trust in God, etc.

Today, they are called Judaism with different branches such as Orthodox, Conservative, Reform, etc. They are the ones who built the Christian Church. They helped to spread the Gospel to the world. When Paul converted to Christianity, he became the slave of Christ Jesus the King.

Before Paul received a fuller truth about the God of Israel, he was a staunch member of the Party of the Pharisees that upheld the Law above everything else. Unfortunately, he was ignorant of the divinity of Christ.

Although a staunch Pharisee, he was really a pagan at heart. He hated Him and His followers so deep and intensely that it turned him into a very dangerous man. He became a murderer of innocent men, women and children whose only crime was deeper search for the God of their ancestor. And Jesus gave them a deeper explanation of who He is. He said that He is in unity with their heavenly Father. Among all the zealot and self-righteous Pharisees, he was the most outstanding in and hard worker. His zeal was too fiery. It blinded him to the truth about the Messiah.

He just went murdering, maiming and imprisoning the Judeo-Christians because he thought they had no right to disagree with him in how to worship the Lord. He terrorized the Christians worship for the glory of God that he never even knew.

One day, he presented himself before the high priests and their lieutenants as the champion for the preservation of the teachings of strict Pharisees like himself taught. He and his fellows were afraid that the teachings they had worked hard to formulate into a strict legal or oral law would disintegrate if Jesus' teachings were allowed to flourish among the Jews. No Christians were allowed to call on God except pure Pharisees and perhaps also the Sadducees and the tax collectors.

The high priests gave him the coveted letters he had begged them to write for him. Some of the letters carried death sentences on the leaders of the infant church in Damascus.

Others contained letters of imprisonment for life for ineffectual Christians. After deposing Church leaders, he would herd the rest like animals back to Jerusalem to face the highest Jewish court in the Holy Land.

Armed with these important letters and well-armed bodyguards, he headed to his Damascus. Though he was Jewish by blood, he was a Hamitic by nationality but from the country of Syria. He was nearing Damascus.

He was excited at the prospect that lay ahead. He would make an example of them that no seed of Abraham was ever again to adopt new teachings that have not been approved by Annas and Caiaphas, the high priests of Israel.

I am Jesus

Someone who is greater than Abraham, the Father of heaven and earth, turned His full light on him. It was so powerful and intense that it knocked Saul off his horse onto the hard ground. He fell fainting to the ground. It took of his breath away. He laid senseless on the ground and half dead.

Then, he heard the most commanding, powerful, awesome and yet musical voice that he had ever heard in his life demanding an immediate answer to His question: "Saul, Saul, why persecutest thou me?" (Acts 9:4).

The heavenly voice asked as to why Saul was beating, lashing, spitting, boxing and was crucifying again and again.

That was not Jewish to slaughter innocent people without a proper trial. The false high priests' henchmen were carrying out the slaughter of their own Jews on the pretext of religious zeal. It was not according to the laws of God and Moses.

Paul wanted to know which one of the Persons in the Triune Godhead was speaking to him. "And he said, Who art thou, Lord?" It was a stupid question. He was killing and imprisoning people without giving each one of them a proper trial. "And the Lord said, I am Jesus whom thou persecutest: it is hard for thee to kick against the pricks" (Acts 9:5).

"I am Jesus. If you believe in Me that I am able to heal you, I will heal you. I am able to save. I am the Son of Man. Above all, "I and my Father are one" (John 10:30).

I am Daddy's Darling Boy. Wherever He goes, I go. Whatever He does, that I also do. He is God in His personality, nature, character and power that also I am. "But Jesus answered them, My Father worketh hitherto, and I work" (John 5:17).

The truth cannot be denied or ignored. I cannot do anything without the loving approval of My Father. Though I am the Almighty Creator God just like My Father, I never do anything to satisfaction of My inner Spirit but for the pleasure of My Father. We do everything together. Whatever He creation He is carrying out, there I am also, working together with Him. We share the same power, authority, love and joy. "Then answered Jesus and said unto them, Verily, verily, I say unto you, The Son can do nothing of himself, but what he seeth the Father do: for what things soever he doeth, these also doeth the Son likewise" (John 5:19).

I am your resurrection. I am your awesome and perfect eternal life. If you have faith and believe that I should find you alive when I come back again, I will find you alive. "Jesus said unto her, I am the resurrection, and the life: he that believeth in me, though he were dead, yet shall he live."

If I find that you have died but had enough faith that I am able to resurrect you from the grave, I will do it for you. I will bring you back to live. "Verily, verily, I say unto you, The hour is coming, and now is, when the dead shall hear the voice of the Son of God: and they that hear shall live" (John 11:25; 5:25).

The President of the Priests or High Priest placed Me under an oath and asked Me to swear before the Almighty God: "I adjure thee by the living God, that thou tell us whether thou be the Christ, the Son of God" (Matthew 26:63).

The High Priest demanded that I swear to the oath if I was the Christ or Savior who was to be sent by God the Father to save the Jews and the whole world from sin and death. I gave Him a strong affirmation that indeed I am. "And Jesus said, I am: and ye shall see the Son of man sitting on the right hand of power, and coming in the clouds of heaven" (Mark 14:62). I am Jesus for whom millions of men, women and children have given up their lives for.

Many more come falling down at my feet and confessing Me as God, King and Lord in submission and confessing their sins. "And Jesus said unto them, I am the bread of life: he that cometh to me shall never hunger; and he that believeth on me shall never thirst" (John 6:35).

I am He who is the Source of Strength that provides eternal life. If you receive My Spirit, you will not die in hell but live forever. Have faith in Me, and I will satisfy your thirst for love, peace, eternal life, joy, etc. "Then spake Jesus again unto them, saying, I am the light of the world: he that followeth me shall not walk in darkness, but shall have the light of life" (John 8:12).

I am the Creative Power that shines with the pure light. I brought existence heaven and the world into existence. I can shine My light in your mind to drive away the darkness of sin and implant My power in you. You will receive new knowledge instead of the knowledge of sin.

My knowledge will help you to protect your life from error and death and guide you in the way of everlasting peace and joy. And I am God the Eternal Father. "Jesus said unto them, Verily, verily, I say unto you, Before Abraham was, I am" (John 8:58).

I am the door for you to receive life everlasting filled with unconditional love, belonging, everlasting friendship, perfect joy, boundless peace and exquisite life. "Then said Jesus unto them again, Verily, verily, I say unto you, I am the door of the sheep.

All that ever came before me are thieves and robbers: but

73

the sheep did not hear them. I am the door: by me if any man enter in, he shall be saved, and shall go in and out, and find pasture" (John 10:7-9).

Anyone who tries to seduce, discourage or drive My children away from Me are thieves and robbers, and I will deal with them. No matter how much a man or woman may be deceived by the devil and his agents, he or she will realize someday and somehow that he or she is sinning by running away from Me. All those who come to Me will blessed more abundantly beyond their wildest dreams.

I am the Creator of life and its full blessings. "The thief cometh not, but for to steal, and to kill, and to destroy: I am come that they might have life, and that they might have it more abundantly" (John 10:10).

I am come to be your full and abundant blessings just as I had planned for you to have before I laid the foundation. I am working on your behalf to recreate you and everything again as you have never fallen in the destructive lifestyle or ever lived in a world gone crazy with sin.

I am the way you should think, talk, and action. I am the truth by which you must live. Anything outside My will is based on the lies of the devil. I am your life. If you wander from Me, you will die the eternal death that will soon take the old world. "Jesus saith unto him, I am the way, the truth, and the life: no man cometh unto the Father, but by me" (John 14:6).

If you come to Me, you are not only coming to Me but to God your Father and God the Holy Spirit. You can see your Father or the Holy Spirit without My permission. I am the King of this world.

You can enter into My kingdom if you accept Me as your personal Savior. Only that way can My blood wash away your sins and infill you with My glory so that you can live with Me.

I am the Root of the Kingdom of David over Israel and the whole world. My kingdom is anchored deep into the earth that no one and even the devil can uproot from power. "I Jesus have sent mine angel to testify unto you these things in the churches. I am the root and the offspring of David, and the bright and morning star" (Revelation 22:16).

Light the bright morning star that heralds the arrival of the morning, I am your light who is heralding the beginning of a new and awesome life for you. I am also the only family tree of King David's family and of the whole world from whom everyone originated and can find meaning and life if he or she wants. "I am the vine, and you are the branches.

If you stay joined to me, and I stay joined to you, then you will produce lots of fruit. But you cannot do anything without me" (John 15:5, CEV).

Another Paul

Raphael, 1483–1520, painted 1515, St Paul Preaching in Athens

Saul was fighting a losing war. "And he said, Who art thou, Lord? And the Lord said, I am Jesus whom thou persecutest: it is hard for thee to kick against the pricks" (Acts 9:5). He implied, "It is very hard, isn't it, for you to lord it over My story." It can also mean: "It is hard for you to lord yourself over Someone who can reduce you to nothing."

Saul was trembling very violently with fear and shock. He was feeling very sick and half dead. He cried deep inside him for mercy and clemency from the Unseen God whose voice boomed from heaven down to earth like the roars of thunders.

He was sure that he was going to die that very moment for all the evil that he had done against Jesus and His household. "And he trembling and astonished said, Lord, what wilt thou have me to do? And the Lord said unto him, Arise, and go into the city, and it shall be told thee what thou must do" (Acts

9:6).

He humbled himself greatly before this Majestic and Awesome Lord whose name He still did not know but was suspicious that He must have been the Resurrected Jesus and Savior of Israel and the whole world. He placed himself at his service at once. He asked the as to what was acceptable to Him that he, Saul, should do for Him.

Sense had, finally, got into Saul's thick head when God roared at him from heaven and knocked him off from his high horse of religious pride and arrogance. Saul had not believed that Jesus had resurrected from the grave. That was why he was mocking the Lord's holy and went about persecuting His followers. But the Lord did rise from the dead.

He confronted His enemy head-on. The collision almost took the life of the foolish man except for the mercy of the ever loving and forgiving God.

Now, Saul had a change of heart after finding out that Jesus does live, and He is very forgiving even to murderers and insolent people like Him who was not just murdering any other people even though that was bad enough but the saints of God.

Saul could now listen to the One he tried to destroy by killing off His followers. Jesus told Saul that he was now married to him and not to his ideologies or theologies. He is God, High Priest and Savior who must be worshipped and served. Allegiance must be rendered to him and not to church leaders such as Caiaphas and Annas.

He is the One who is directing his own affairs. He is neither tutored nor ordered around by neither religious sect such as of the Pharisees, Sadducees, Essenes, etc. or by political parties such as the Romans, Herodians, etc.

He was told to go to the city to receive the remainder of his blessings which would instruct him what to do for the glory of One he tried to murder through his disciples. His first blessing was the head-on collision with God that saved his life from eternal ruin and the deaths of many innocent saints. He was humbled very terribly. He was ordered to meet not the high priests in Jerusalem but the very man he was going to murder in Damascus.

He would be taught the real truth concerning the Creator,

His incarnation into the human race, work, death, resurrection and soon Second Coming in power and glory to receive the world back into His kingdom. He would be given proper instructions in how he must humble himself completely before the Holy One.

He would be taught how to worship Him right in order help him to serve the Lord with all his mind, heart, spirit and power. The Lord had shown great mercies to him. He has been very good to Him by coming in person to witness about Himself that He is God Almighty of Abraham, Isaac and Jacob. And it is only civil that he should render the very best services he could master in His honor.

He must not be lazy or slow about it but must move very fast as a missionary to Israel and the whole world. He was to rebuke their sins and speak comfortingly to hearts that are broken and urge all of them to come back to God their Father.

He would restore them to their lost estate. They would once again become His glorious, eternal and powerful sons and daughters. "But unto you that fear my name shall the Sun of righteousness arise with healing in his wings; and ye shall go forth, and grow up as calves of the stall" Malachi 4:2).

Anyone who keeps the Holy Spirit in his or heart as the most precious treasure on earth shall be saved. Live within the arms of the Almighty One. Receive your life from Him with thanksgiving and praises.

He is the Father of righteousness and perfect holiness. He has compassion and tender love for all of you. He is overshadowing you with eternal healings for your body and spirit. Have faith in Him and keep His commandments holy. You will fly away from this earth to heaven like galloping young and powerful horses.

The bodyguards and fellow travelers of Saul were thunderstruck with shock and amazement during this show of power between heaven and their companion. They also had seen the beautiful light of heaven and heard the majestic voice but saw no visible form of the Speaker.

They knew that it was none other but God Himself talking to Saul. They stood around the man they had feared and adored in shock and amazement. He was the leader of their group but now he was lying on his face on the ground fainting, helpless and weeping.

He had no strength. So they helped him to rise up. He had gone completely blind. The glory of Jesus was so bright that it scorched the eyes of Saul. He went totally blind. They led the once mighty man by hand and into the city.

The Lord spoke with the spirit of Ananias in a form of a vision. He told him to go to a house standing on Straight Street. A man by the name of Saul was under his orders to receive healing and missionary work.

This very man, indeed, was in prayers and fasting for miracles for his blinded eyes and work to do for the Lord. He spent three days and three nights fasting, praying, weeping and repenting of all the murderers and atrocities he did against God and against the church.

Ananias feared that he was walking into the lion's jaws. Many people had told him that Saul had performed many and great demoniac works against the saints in Jerusalem and was now come to Damascus to continue His evil work against the church. But the Lord assured him that he was now a changed man.

Ananias was to go on His behalf and speak to the man who now was begging to be one of them. He would be the brain behind the work of lifting up His "But the Lord said unto him, Go thy way: for he is a chosen vessel unto me, to bear my name before the Gentiles, and kings, and the children of Israel" (Acts 9:15).

Saul would be greatly humbled and emptied of his human pride and egotism because the Lord's name would be very sweet in his heart, and he would never stop declaring that Jesus is Lord. He would raise up offsprings the world over for the Lord His God.

The Lord asked Ananias to please kindly forgive the man who had wanted to kill him but to go and pray over him and heal his eyesores. "And Ananias went his way, and entered into the house; and putting his hands on him said, Brother Saul, the Lord, even Jesus, that appeared unto thee in the way as thou camest, hath sent me, that thou mightest receive thy sight, and be filled with the Holy Ghost. And immediately there fell from his eyes as it had been scales: and he received sight forthwith, and arose, and was baptized" (Acts 9:17, 18).

Paul converted into Christianity and was now living a life of faith based on the blood of Jesus Christ your Lord and Master. He won his heart. He was very happy and content to be the Lord's prisoner of love. He was a happy slave of the Messiah who took him away from a life of murders, blasphemes, threats, imprisonments, etc. of Christians.

Christian faith demands a Christ-like character at all times. It is practical Christianity washed in the blood of Christ, led by the Holy Spirit and walking the way of sanctification that is guided by the Ten Commandments.

From then on Saul was a changed man. The Pharisee was now known as Paul, the missionary to Israel and the whole world. He said he was the cream of all the Pharisees because he did everything exactly as ordered on all Jews by the traditions of their fathers. "Circumcised the eighth day, of the stock of Israel, of the tribe of Benjamin, an Hebrew of the Hebrews; as touching the law, a Pharisee; Concerning zeal, persecuting the church; touching the righteousness which is in the law, blameless" (Philippians 3:5).

He said that he was a circumcised Jew according to the law given to Abraham and his descendants. He was from the tribe of Israel and clan of Benjamin. He was the best Hebrews not just but blood but he kept all the traditional laws of the fathers or the oral laws. And that meant that He was a good Pharisee that kept the oral laws and Mosaic laws. To keep those additional laws beside the Ten Commandments meant that he was a true Israeli above none practicing Israelis.

And as a true Jew, he was zealous for their traditional laws. He was angry with the Christians for not obeying them. They were not good Jews. They were not living according to the oral laws handed down to them by their ancestors. They were lawless but he was blames, perfect, and righteous.

Since they refused to be Jews by obeying the traditions of the fathers and instead believed in Jesus, he went out imprisoning and murdering them in the name of the laws of their fathers. But he changed when he met Jesus. He was now the follower of the Son of God.

No one had produced greater results for the work of the Lord Jesus Christ than Paul. He was humbled many times very humble for the sake of the Lord he loved very much. Paul listed some of his suffering so that you may hear about the Gospel of Jesus Christ and be saved.

He said that you may think that he was brain dead for suffering for you so much when he did not even know you. But he wants to assure that his sufferings were worth it. You need to know, love and serve Jesus like He did because He is all that you got and nothing else.

He labored day and night without rest for your sake and much more for the sake of Jesus Christ your Father and Savior. He suffered very greatly and countless of times more than words can described. For countless of times, men had would remove their leather belts and beat him with.

There were some official floggings he received by the orders of the Jewish religious courts. "Are they ministers of Christ? (I speak as a fool) I am more; in labours more abundant, in stripes above measure, in prisons more frequent, in deaths oft. Of the Jews five times received I forty stripes save one" (2 Corinthians 11:23, 24).

His persecutors were none other than his fellow Pharisees and some of the Sadducees whom he knew very well. They gave him 39 x 5 = 195 floggings in total. He was a frequent jailbird. He was often beaten and left for the dead.

The Pharisees and Sadducees were sitting in court against Saint Paul for preaching that the Messiah was the Sent of God. He came down on earth, suffered, and died to save Israel and the whole world. But the leaders murdered Him. They did not want to be called murderers.

They were determined to make an example of Paul, too, because He kept saying that the Messiah had risen from the dead. It meant that they would come into the judgment hall of God and must answer to what they did to Him. "But when Paul perceived that the one part were Sadducees, and the other Pharisees, he cried out in the council, Men and brethren, I am a Pharisee, the son of a Pharisee: of the hope and resurrection of the dead I am called in question.

And when he had so said, there arose a dissension between the Pharisees and the Sadducees: and the multitude was divided. For the Sadducees say that there is no resurrection, neither angel, nor spirit: but the Pharisees confess both.

And there arose a great cry: and the scribes that were of the Pharisees' part arose, and strove, saying, We find no evil in this man: but if a spirit or an angel hath spoken to him, let us not fight against God. And when there arose a great dissension, the chief captain, fearing lest Paul should have been pulled in pieces of them, commanded the soldiers to go down, and to take him by force from among them, and to bring him into the castle" (Acts 23:6–10). That day, the Pharisees saved Paul from being murdered because he was their fellow Pharisee.

He went on to list some of his suffering he had to endure so that you may hear the Gospel of your Messiah. "Thrice was I beaten with rods. ..." The rods with which he was beaten were used in such a way that each that he was lashed it would go round his body like being clothed in a garment. "Thrice was I beaten with rods, once was I stoned, thrice I suffered shipwreck, a night and a day I have been in the deep" (2 Corinthians 11:25).

When he was stoned but thank God he fainted. He was left for the dead. The Lord saved his life and he walked away alive. His body was broken and wounded by shipwrecks. During one of the shipwrecks, he had to swim all night and all day long before he found land.

He was always on a safari to preach the word of God. The countries were wilder then compared to this present time. They were no good roads. The ships were death coffins. Come some storms, they can break easily and sink into the depth of the sea and cause countless loss of lives. They were pirates to face in the open sea and robbers lurking around on the dry land.

He pointed out the difficulties of traveling in those days: "In journeyings often, in perils of waters, in perils of robbers, in perils by mine own countrymen, in perils by the heathen, in perils in the city, in perils in the wilderness, in perils in the sea, in perils among false brethren" (2 Corinthians 11:26).

In addition to all the above mentioned problems, he had often been branded by some ignorant Jews who had not met their Messiah that he as a destroyer of their Jewish faith. He was often outraised or flogged by the people he loved and was trying to reach with the Gospel of their own God. He suffered because of the lies that some people were spreading about him.

But people who were the worst to him were the pagans. Many of them were very dangerous people who trusted no one and not even themselves. The Roman soldiers were always on the move and so were the other nations and kingdoms. Wars and revolts were frequent.

People did not trust each other. But the Lord was calling them to come to Him. And he went to preach to them the Good News that would give them peace and hope for an eternal future. The metropolitan cities and towns were centers of corruptions, violence and lynching. They had tried to lynch him many times. They had imprisoned him many times.

Robbers and thieves infested where there were lawlessness, poverty, diseases, etc. abounded. He was in fear of his life all the time but pushed on for your sake and the sake of Christ your God and King. As he had pointed out before, traveling by sea meant taking ships.

They were by themselves death-traps. They were weak and most often did not have the strength to withstand the storms of the sea. And above all these sufferings none hurt him more than bad Christians who spread false reports about him.

They cut deep into his heart. Only the grace of God kept him forgiving and loving them and pushing ever forward into new frontiers to preach the word of truth.

His sufferings, rejections, beatings, painful body, etc. were more than he could bear except for the grace of God that kept him moving ever forward with courage and boldness to always preach the word of life to all those who were willing to hear him. He kept constant vigil over his life like a soldier on 24 hours duty or he could have died long ago in the hands of some people.

It also helped him to be praying all the time just praying and worshipping his God and your God. Many times, he had gone without food and water for days on end. Though he often went hungry or barely had enough to eat, he did not excuse himself from fasting. He fasted often for the spread of the Gospel and that you, too, may learn about it and love it like he did. His strength of keeping alive was the Lord and no one else.

He, often, wore torn and tattered clothing because he could not afford new ones. And no one took pity on him and gave him any hand-me-downs. "In weariness and painfulness, in watchings often, in hunger and thirst, in fastings often, in cold and nakedness" (2 Corinthians 11:27). He had no coverings at night and during winter times but bore the cold bravely in order that you may, one day, learn about Jesus and He will save you.

As if these problems were not enough, he had to worry about the spiritual and social progress of the churches that he had raised. Wolves were sneaking into the churches and stealing the sheep. They were scattering and confusing the saints with strange doctrines.

They only wanted leadership in the churches and were not after winning souls and uplifting the name of the Messiah. And these kinds of people hurt him more than the ignorant Pharisees and Sadducees concerning the truths and faith of the Lord the Messiah.

He feared them more than thieves, robbers, hunger, thirst, beatings, imprisonments, nakedness, etc. He prayed for the spiritual, mental and social progress of the churches and visited the members whenever he could to encourage and strengthen them in the Lord.

He said, "Beside those things that are without, that which cometh upon me daily, the care of all the churches" (2 Corinthians 11:28).

Some of you may think that you have suffered too much for the Lord. You are claiming that you are giving up too much for Him and you are having about enough of Him. Paul is begging you not to give up on your Lord.

He gave up important positions in the sect of the Pharisees. "I am verily a man which am a Jew, born in Tarsus, a city in Cilicia, yet brought up in this city at the feet of Gamaliel, and taught according to the perfect manner of the law of the fathers, and was zealous toward God, as ye all are this day. And profited in the Jews' religion above many my equals in mine own nation, being more exceedingly zealous of the traditions of my fathers" (Acts 22:3; Galatians 1:14).

He graduated from the outstanding and highly acclaimed

University of Jerusalem under the professorship of Gamaliel with high honors. He was well versed in the orals laws or traditions handed down by the sages of Israel which they had considered were more important than the Ten Commandments and laws of Moses.

For if Israel kept them correct, then they were keeping the Law of God right. Their salvation was based on keeping the traditions of the fathers correctly and not by faith in the blood of Christ.

He was a scholar of the highest caliber in those teachings and no one could argue with them or defeat him in his reasons of what he taught was the best education in the world. His fellow graduates from the University of Jerusalem could not present sound sermons and arguments like him.

And of course some of you think that serving the Lord and/or living a decent Christian life is making you poorer by the day. You are almost ready to give up on God because of your poverty and suffering.

Paul said that he, too, gave up a good business for the sake of the Lord. Had he stayed in one place and carried on with his business of making tents, he would have been a very rich and wealthy man. But he usually made and sold enough materials for his next meal and to pay for his travels in spreading the Gospel.

But he often pushed on "In weariness and painfulness, in watchings often, in hunger and thirst, in fastings often, in cold and nakedness" (2 Corinthians 11:27). He endured all of these things and much more because the love of Christ is stronger than physical, security, social, political, educational, economical, etc. needs.

Are you beaten, rejected, outraised, poor, etc. for Christ's sake? Paul said that you are not alone. "Who is weak, and I am not weak? who is offended, and I burn not?" 2 Corinthians 11:29).

It is not easy being a loner because you want to always do that which is right. Human beings are created to have companies and belongings. They thrive best in the sunshine of love and appreciations. But He who created your heart knows what is best for it. And the best thing for it is Christ Himself. Things of this world may come and gone but Christ promised to be your Eternal Lover.

Paul said that he was not ashamed for being a weak human being. It meant that he needed the All-Powerful Christ. "And he said unto me, My grace is sufficient for thee: for my strength is made perfect in weakness. Most gladly therefore will I rather glory in my infirmities, that the power of Christ may rest upon me. Therefore I take pleasure in infirmities, in reproaches, in necessities, in persecutions, in distresses for Christ's sake: for when I am weak, then am I strong" (2 Corinthians 12:9, 10).

May be your humanity has other afflictions such as some handicaps, diseases, poverty, loneliness, etc. Your sufferings are not necessarily death sentences by themselves. They are obstacles that you must conquer and win the crown of life. In spite of them, you can win in this world and conquer whatever you set your mind to do.

Paul was clinically blind, that is, he could see for a short distance but not far away. He could hardly read even his own manuscripts. Other people had to write things for him. He dictated his letters and signed his name on them. "And lest I should be exalted above measure through the abundance of the revelations, there was given to me a thorn in the flesh, the messenger of Satan to buffet me, lest I should be exalted above measure. For this thing I besought the Lord thrice, that it might depart from me" (2 Corinthians 12:7, 8).

In spite of his blindness, Paul wrote more books in the New Testament than the Lord's disciples did. He reasoned better than even Abraham, Moses, King David, etc. He is the best theologians born among men and women on earth. Yet, he was a blind man.

He was beaten and imprisoned so many times that he became physically weak. He said, "If I must needs glory, I will glory of the things which concern mine infirmities. The God and Father of our Lord Jesus Christ, which is blessed for evermore, knoweth that I lie not." (2 Corinthians 11:30, 31).

Like Paul, rejoice in your infirmities in that they are giving you the chances to receive double glories than people who think that they are normal and have everything they need, and so they have succeeded. But you do not have all the blessings of this world but in spite of that you have succeeded in knowing Christ and witnessing for Him.

You are spiritually strengthened and you want to do some other things for Him and for yourself and your family just go ahead and do them. Limitations should challenge you to excel even more. As a human being, you have more gut in side you than hunger, thirst, diseases, handicaps of this kind of that kind, poverty, racism, nepotism, persecutions, etc.

You can excel in anything if you put your mind into. And with the help of Christ, you are already a conqueror. Go out and receive your successes that have already been won on the Cross of Calvary.

Christ encourages you to leave everything in His hands. "And he said unto me, My grace is sufficient for thee: for my strength is made perfect in weakness. Most gladly therefore will I rather glory in my infirmities, that the power of Christ may rest upon me" (2 Corinthians 12:9).

It is the Spirit of Christ that is more powerful than your physical, social, financial, political, etc. handicaps. So you remain without excuse if you do not do those things which He has called you out to perform for His name's sake and perfect glory.

Christ loves you whether you are a sinner or saint. Physical, social, religious, economic, political, etc. hardships are temporal. They have failed to come between great spiritual man like Paul and they will definitely fail to come between you and the Christ that you love. "Who shall separate us from the love of Christ? shall tribulation, or distress, or persecution, or famine, or nakedness, or peril, or sword?" (Romans 8:35).

Who receives people so lovingly, tenderly and with complete pardon for all their sins and weaknesses like Christ their God, Creator and King? He made them for love and joy. He alone understands why they weak and how to help them regain their power over sin, death, nature and demons. Troubles come to all the living on the earth. Only the dead are resting in peace.

Many problems often come unexpected and sudden. When you are in Christ, He will hold your heart in His tender, steady and strong hand during times of troubles, suffering and death. He is always with you the storms hate, wars, persecutions, poverty, loneliness, depressions, hunger, thirst, etc. are beating upon you very mercilessly.

People as well as nature may try to show that they are more powerful than you are but do not faint with fear. God is with you. There are dangers everywhere at home and outside. You may fall on some sharp objects at home and die. Something may fall on you and crush you to death if you go outside. But Christ is with you wherever you may be. You got to live, enjoy life and excel in spite of these dangers.

The life of a Christian is in constant danger because Satan is angry with Christ. "As it is written, For thy sake we are killed all the day long; we are accounted as sheep for the slaughter" (Romans 8:36). Since Satan cannot hurt or kill God, he has turn his anger on you.

He has tried to erase the Judeo-Christian people from the earth but they are the stronger for it. "Nay, in all these things we are more than conquerors through him that loved us" (Romans 8:37).

When the devil has forced you to go down the sea, you must swim right up and back to the surface of the water. Do not give in and drown in your problems. You have no right to commit suicide. Life is sacred. It belongs to God and must be protected, loved and petted with good people and stuff whenever possible.

You are the Creator's baby. No parent hurts more than when his or her helpless baby is in agony. God is the best Daddy and of all good daddies and the best Mom of all good mothers. He hurts very deeply when you are hurting. Though saints are dying all the time, the living ones among them have not given up the desire to live and excel whenever possible. Christ lives in your to excel in whatever you want to do here on earth and especially when you arrive home safe in heaven.

Unhindered by personal sins and weaknesses by the harassments of demons, sicknesses and diseases, you will be a huge success. It is the Lord Himself who declares that you are going to be really great. He will place you in charge of his household as a junior god, king/queen and lord.

Death may dog your footsteps all the time but you are a not a defeat. You are a winner. You have gut, and you will conquer all sins, weakness, death, etc. by the power of the Lord your God. "For I am persuaded, that neither death, nor life, nor angels, nor principalities, nor powers, nor things present, nor things to come, Nor height, nor depth, nor any other creature, shall be able to separate us from the love of God, which is in Christ Jesus our Lord" (Romans 8:38, 39).

You have come into this world to stay. Death cannot make a full end of you. You will resurrect right back to life from the grave. Life with all its problems is no problems at all. They will pass but you will endure in Christ forever. No holy angel is greater than you in anything.

You are both sons and daughters of God Almighty with equal rights before Him. No devil is more powerful than you. With a prayer, you will always drive them away. One day, you will see them meet their end when they will be burnt up. You will come on top of them as a great conqueror.

Earthly positions in the families, churches, governments, companies, etc. are temporary measurements. In a way, they are artificial. They are there to help lead the world out of the present dilemma caused by sin. No powers on earth such as political, military, economic, social, etc. can control your mind and heart. You are not inferior to any leader or powerful people on earth.

You are not born according to the dictates of this world but because God wanted you for a baby. "But as many as received him, to them gave he power to become the sons of God, even to them that believe on his name: Which were born, not of blood, nor of the will of the flesh, nor of the will of man, but of God" (John 1:12, 13). Therefore, none of the powers and/or leaders of this world must make you turn your back on your beloved Christ and King. Obey no orders except that of God your Father.

The powers of this present world order cannot force you to abandon faith. You are stronger than all of them. Their guns, imprisonments, tortures, etc. cannot make you to be less than whom you have chosen to be, that is, like Jesus Christ.

Future events are going to be worse than the present ones during the time when the world will come to her final end. Even they cannot change you to be a whiner, weakling or beast. You are being absorbed into the supernatural life of Christ and will always stand strong for Him.

No angel in heaven or devil in hell must never be able persuade you leave Christ your Savior. No angel, human being, animal, bird, fish, etc. have power control over your mind and heart. They must come between you and your Savior. You are under God and no one else. The Spirit of the Unconquerable is working in you.

The human race was defeated by the devil and sin but it is not down and out because no one can defeat God residing in them. It cannot be overwhelmed by defeats, sin and death. And you are one of them who continue to live in spite of the shadow of troubles and death hanging over them all the time.

You are already a conqueror of the whole world. You are the god, king/queen and lord of heaven and all the universes under the God of gods, King of kings and Lord of lords. You are in the arms of divine love that heavily lashed in Christ your Lord. "Blessed be the God and Father of our Lord Jesus Christ, who hath blessed us with all spiritual blessings in heavenly places in Christ: According as he hath chosen us in him before the foundation of the world, that we should be holy and without blame before him in love: Having predestinated us unto the adoption of children by Jesus Christ to himself, according to the good pleasure of his will" (Ephesians 1:3–5).

God your Father has poured on you the kind of life the Second Godhead, Jesus Christ, is enjoying in heaven. He blessed you with that kind of life before the foundation of the earth. It is time that you must rise up in faith and receive. Very soon, Christ appears in full glory, it will become a reality in your life. You are His child, and He wants you to be like Him in appearance, thought, speech, power, grace, etc.

If there is room in the heart of God for Paul the murderer and persecutor of the saints, there is room for you, too. He died for bad people. If you are decent according to worldly standard, you are still a bad person in God's sight.

Come to Him and be saved. "I am crucified with Christ: nevertheless I live; yet not I, but Christ liveth in me: and the life which I now live in the flesh I live by the faith of the Son of God, who loved me, and gave himself for me" (Galatians 2:20).

You have been crucified together with Christ your Father more than two thousand years ago. You are no longer a sinner but a saint. You are not your own boss but a servant of Christ your Maker. You cannot give brainpower for your mind to think, make your heart beat, blood flow, etc.

Everything in you belongs to your Maker. And the present body has been crucified on the Cross of Calvary so that you can receive the everlasting life of God in a new and indestructible body. Jesus is still living and walking around in this world. He is living in you. Continue to live by faith and you will soon receive your new body and spirit from your Messiah. He gave over His body to death so that you may receive His eternal Spirit in yourself and live ever abundantly and wonderfully forever.

6 CHAPTER

WOES ON PHARISEES

1. Woes on Pharisees, lawyers, scribes, etc.

The Messiah spoke not only to the Jews of His day but to all Christendom. He warned all of you against being hypocrites, legalists, agnostics, and atheists out of His great compassion and love.

He wanted to save them from their pitfalls and foolishness of the Pharisees, teachers of the Law, and lawyers or defenders of the Judaism. He wanted to cut short their sins and introduce holiness in their hearts. He felt that He had an obligation to save them because they were the people who came out of Himself.

And now He had selected some of them to be His disciples to spread His message of love, hope, salvation, etc. to all parts of the world. "Then spake Jesus to the multitude, and to his disciples, Saying, The scribes and the Pharisees sit in Moses' seat: All therefore whatsoever they bid you observe, that observe and do; but do not ye after their works: for they say, and do not" (Matthew 23:1–3).

He was saying, "I am the Lawgiver. It was My chair that Moses was sitting on when he was teaching Israel about the Moral Law. I sent him also to teach the other laws such as the ceremonial, health, social, etc. laws. And now the scribes and Pharisees are sitting on Moses' chair that I had leant to him to teach you briefly on My behalf.

All of you must listen carefully and obey everything they are teaching you out of the Law. Keep the word in your heart and guard it very all your mind and strength. Whatever they tell you from the Bible that it is important to keep, better obey it. It is important. But that are dark and sinful activities in their accounts.

Do not commit them simply because your priests, scribes, church defenders or lawyers, etc. are committing them. Some of their hypocrisy is plain and some are not. Obey only the things that are in the Bible that they are teaching you but do not live like them. Live like God."

The Messiah commends Jews and Gentile Christians for joining His priesthood and for doing various works in the church for Him. He is their High Priest. But He warns everyone from diverting from His plain teachings and preaching heresies instead. "For they bind heavy burdens and grievous to be borne, and lay them on men's shoulders; but they themselves will not move them with one of their fingers" (Matthew 23:4).

Man-made laws are burdensome because they do not bring peace and joy into the heart. They are not creative words that can bring changes in human souls. As such, they are too difficult to obey and even to remember the whole list. They are too heavy.

They crush the spirits of men and women and make wastes out of their lives. But the hypocritical Bible teachers are very unsympathetic. They are abusive in their statements and manners towards Christians who have failed to obey all their man-made doctrines, rules, and regulations. They would not touch these fallen sinners with their fingers. They would not teach them the plain word of God in order to cheer up their spirits.

Hypocrites force other people to be good Christians while they themselves are as weak as the rest of the community of faith and the pagans. They are intolerant and mean towards the failings of other Christians. They speak about laws and rules but are break them.

When they are caught, they make excuses and shed crocodile tears but have no true heart conversion. They make

Christian look boring or downright difficult. They make rules to circumvent the truths of God that they do not want to obey. They uphold their theologies over the plain word of the Lord just like the Pharisees who preferred their own laws above everything else.

But once God's word drops into the soul, it may remain dormant for many years but one day, it will germinate, pop up a seedling, and grow into a full tree of righteousness. God alone can create people. He is the only one to make decrees as laws for the people to follow so that they can find peace, happiness, and eternity.

The Law of God is as eternal as Himself. But human laws have beginnings. They can change. Therefore, they cannot bring eternal stability in human lives. The Law explains how to worship and love God and how to love other people. The goal of the Law is to bring peace and joy in the practitioner. It will bring a new creation in the body and spirit of the follower.

But human rules are formulated for the purpose of self-promotions and not for the genuine love of God. "But all their works they do for to be seen of men: they make broad their phylacteries, and enlarge the borders of their garments" (Matthew 23:5).

Always check yourself to see that what you are saying or doing for God is not to attract attention to yourself. Your clothing, food, water, etc. should not be displayed in excessive manners in order to draw applause from fellow Christians that you are very spiritual. Acting as a spiritual man or woman is a common affliction in mankind. The truth is that they are sinners. But pray all the time as your preach and/work for Him to keep you humble.

The people are not foolish. They will sense if you proud. They will spoil the weak by your sinfulness. You will discourage those who are committed to the Lord. They may turn away from Him because you are full of darkness.

You have shut out the light that could have pointed Christ to them. If you are an attention getter, you have missed the mark. You are on your own.

The Messiah is not with you. Everyone craves for love and belonging. But be careful not to take the place of the Messiah in order to find love, belonging, and praises for yourself.

Everyone who takes the name of God as his or her Savior is a spiritual man or woman. It is good to be spiritual. You are changing and becoming like God. And there are people who give special reverence to spiritual people.

Once in a while, they may treat with reverence and respect. But do not allow it to get into your head. It will make your life miserable when they do not treat your right. As a spiritual man or woman, do not look for the honor and respect everywhere you go. Be humble and accept they good and bad ways people treat you with humility.

Hypocrites suffer from feelings inferiority complex. They will be upset if they are not treated rights. They are always dying to be recognized as spiritual men and women. "And love the uppermost rooms at feasts, and the chief seats in the synagogues" (Matthew 23:6).

The only Person who has the first place in heaven and on the earth is God the Father. Even the Almighty Son and the Holy Spirit are under His authority. He is asking you to hand over first places to Him. It belongs to Him whether they are in the church, weddings, funerals, etc.

You are just a servant. Take whatever seat that is available in the church or social gatherings. Do not feel humiliated. You are in the service of the First Godhead, even God your Father. He will give you peace and joy more than the people who are showing off in the meetings against you. You will walk away with your head held high.

God has the first place in the hearts of all converts. If they refuse not to recognize your presence, you are really not that important. You are not their Life Giver. God has first place in their hearts or some other personal ambitions. So do not weep, mourn and cry about love lost and honors withheld. If they do not call you a holy man or woman, it is alright.

If they do not call you a pastor, rabbi, deacon, deaconess, teach, doctor, nurse, etc. it is alright. Do not take it to heart. The real pastor, rabbi, deacon, deaconess, teacher, doctor, nurse, etc. is God.

Direct their minds to Him if you see that they are worshipping you because you are very good to them. "And greetings in the markets, and to be called of men, Rabbi,

Rabbi. But be not yet called Rabbi: for one is your Master, even Christ; and all ye are brethren" (Matthew 23:7, 8).

God is the Savior and Helper of the world. You must not allow yourself to be called the Savior. He is the Lord and the Helper of all. Accept the lowly name of a servant or slave.

Tell them because you are the servant or slave of God, that is why you are also their servant or slave. "But he that is greatest among you shall be your servant" (Matthew 23:11).

That is the mark of true greatness. There is only one Teacher of righteousness here in this world. He is the Messiah and God of all. You are all equal in this world. Both teachers and students are brothers and sisters.

God is the Father of heaven and earth. Make sure that you are not enslaving anyone spiritually, socially, emotionally, etc. to call you Master or behave towards like a slave. Do not be like Satan who is enslaving the world and murdering them day and night. There is only one Master on earth. He is the Messiah. He is the Master of creation and salvation.

He is their Master of love, joy, peace, eternal life, etc. "And call no man your father upon the earth: for one is your Father, which is in heaven. Neither be ye called masters: for one is your Master, even Christ" (Matthew 23:9, 10).

Self-exaltation comes natural because of the sinful weaknesses of the flesh. But the Lord has promised to make the hearts of believers humble, decent and holy. Pride leads to nowhere. It breeds enmity between you and people. God will despise you, too. "Though He scoffs at the scoffers and scorns the scorners, yet He gives His undeserved favor to the low [in rank], the humble, and the afflicted. [James 4:6; I Pet. 5:5.]" (Proverbs 3:34, AMP).

The only thing that is highly exalted in this world is the Gospel and not human ideas, philosophies, wealth, physique, powers, etc. "And whosoever shall exalt himself shall be abased; and he that shall humble himself shall be exalted" (Matthew 23:12).

The Gospel will triumph at the end of the world but all human laws, fame, riches, etc. will turn into dust. But anyone who humbles himself or herself and exalts the Gospel of the Messiah instead will be exalted on the Day of Judgment. He or she will receive the crown of life. You are the slave of the

Gospel. Serve Him with humility and love, and He will bless you.

Many people know the Bible very well. There are thousands of excellent Bible scholars in all Christian churches and the different branches of Judaism. If only their knowledge could match their spirituality, the whole world will be filled with the Presence of God.

Miracles will be occurring every day. The blind will see. The deaf will hear. The dumb will speak. Handicaps will be made whole. The dead will rise from the dead. But alas! The majority of them have head knowledge only. Their hearts are not filled with the Holy Spirit. They know God but they cannot sense His Presence in their daily lives.

The Messiah says of them, "But woe unto you, scribes and Pharisees, hypocrites! for ye shut up the kingdom of heaven against men: for ye neither go in yourselves, neither suffer ye them that are entering to go in" (Matthew 23:13).

Bible scholars or scribes know God but they do not want Him as a personal Friend and Savior. They show off when they are teaching people about God. They are resisting the influences of the Holy Spirit. They do not want to enter into friendship, grace, and love of God. They discourage others by their actions to come to God. They will be sorry for losing such a great salvation.

In Middle East, it is common to hear someone showing off saying, "I will show you." Some people will do very bad things and will boast, "I showed you."

Most people in Middle East like to show off that they are strong, powerful, intelligent, educated, wise, etc. Everyone is somebody. If you cross their path, they will show you something to let you know that they are also important just like you or even better. They like giving their opinions in meetings.

They are really good people at heart but you have to allow them to express themselves or you will make them nervous. They will be suspicious of your intentions if they do not have a voice. They do not enjoy backing down to give place to someone else for fear that people will take advantage of them and humiliate them all their lives.

It is these kind of people that the Messiah called the show

offs. It is what English translation called the hypocrites. "Woe unto you, scribes and Pharisees, hypocrites! for ye devour widows' houses, and for a pretence make long prayer: therefore ye shall receive the greater damnation" (Matthew 23:14).

Most hypocrites love money. Since they have rejected the peace and joy of God, they are turning to this world to find some meaning for their lives. Some turn to money, worldly successes, fame, etc.

They will not forgive debts of dead people whose widows and children are suffering terribly. They will get everything out of the widows and even drive them out of their lands and houses in order to get profits.

The Bible scholars and Pharisees showed off to the people that they were learnt in the Word of God. They wanted people to take note that they were very spiritual and holy people by offering long prayers, fasting two days a week, etc.

Hypocrites are also good evangelists. "Woe unto you, scribes and Pharisees, hypocrites! for ye compass sea and land to make one proselyte, and when he is made, ye make him twofold more the child of hell than yourselves" (Matthew 23:15).

But why doesn't the Messiah appreciate the works of hypocrites bringing lost sinners into the church on His behalf? They like to give orders which they themselves do not like to obey. Hypocrites and legalists love to preach. They love missionary work. They will go all over the land and overseas to look for converts.

Unfortunately, they have neither known nor understood who God really is. They have no idea how to live by the Law of love. They do not live by faith in the righteousness of the blood of Christ. They trust in salvation by own works. They convert people who will trust in salvation by works. These converts are narrow-minded bigots.

No matter how much you preach to them about salvation by faith in blood of Christ, they will not believe you. They are twice children of hell than the people who converted into the Church. They are twice dead than the legalist or hypocritical missionaries.

The priests, Bible teachers, defenders of the church,

lawyers, and etc. duty are to lead the flock to the Messiah. But if they do not know Him, they will all fall into the pit of errors and hell. One the greatest problem facing Christians and the Church is how to handle finances.

The church must pay bills and the salaries of her workers. But the money must be obtained and invested wisely and for the glory of the great Giver. There is nothing in this world that belongs to anyone. They all belong to the Creator.

Because of the upheavals of the financial market, it is easy to be carried away in trying to get every dollar for the use of the Church or for personal or for personal use in dubious ways. Money is considered to be more important than the Church. And when it is considered so, it is placed above God.

The Messiah rebukes blind devotion to wealth. "Woe unto you, ye blind guides, which say, Whosoever shall swear by the temple, it is nothing; but whosoever shall swear by the gold of the temple, he is a debtor! Ye fools and blind: for whether is greater, the gold, or the temple that sanctifieth the gold? And,

Whosoever shall swear by the altar, it is nothing; but whosoever sweareth by the gift that is upon it, he is guilty. Ye fools and blind: for whether is greater, the gift, or the altar that sanctifieth the gift?

Whoso therefore shall swear by the altar, sweareth by it, and by all things thereon. And whoso shall swear by the temple, sweareth by it, and by him that dwelleth therein. And he that shall swear by heaven, sweareth by the throne of God, and by him that sitteth thereon" (Matthew 23:16–22).

People who do not have God in their hearts have not met Him. They are spiritually blind. They glory in their churches and their achievements. But the Lord wants you to turn away your eyes from your impressive churches and their achievements, properties, financial successes, etc.

The Church is the holy temple of the Lord. The furniture, equipment, gold, money, etc. of the Church are holy because of the Presence of the Holy One who lives in her. He is above them all. People should love Him more than what the Church has. All her things will pass away but God lives on forever.

He is the true Church and not buildings, money, businesses, schools, hospitals, ministries, professions, etc. You are alive because of Him. You will be saved from this hell by

His power. You will not be saved by what your Church is or what she can do.

God appreciates your tithes of even negligible things such as a pinch of salt, spice, herb, etc. He does not demand that you must pay tithes of insignificant things like very small garden herbs you grew in small pot. You may have harvested only give leaves. But if you want to tithe it, He will smile at your strict way of offering Him services.

Important as giving tithes and offerings are, He said that He will love you more if you will put love first. Love Him first, others second, and yourself love. That is what will save you from this world and not the tithing and offerings though important they are to Him and to the Church. "Woe unto you, scribes and Pharisees, hypocrites! for ye pay tithe of mint and anise and cummin, and have omitted the weightier matters of the law, judgment, mercy, and faith: these ought ye to have done, and not to leave the other undone" (Matthew 23:23).

The Messiah wants you to live by the truth. He wants you to be merciful to lost sinners, the weak, sick, suffering, etc. and give them sympathetic words. He wants you to help them whenever possible. He wants you to live by faith in the blood He has shed for you. It will wash away your sins, build His character in you, and create a new body and spirit in you.

Judges are the guides of blind sinners. They teach the Law and the righteousness of God to sinners. They lead them by example in obeying the Law of heaven. But if the judges of the land are blind, the sinners will remain blind. They will never find God their Savior. Judges who only spell out judgments against offenders are not helping them find the Messiah. Every Christian is a judge.

Do not try to live by the Law and forget how to love God and sinners. "Ye blind guides, which strain at a gnat, and swallow a camel" (Matthew 23:24).

Legalism is making sure there is no a single chemical in your water. Straining all chemicals from your water is almost impossible. When you forget the Law of love you are swallowing many camel-size sins. They will kill you.

God can create spirits, matter, space, time, righteousness, holiness, etc. Human beings cannot create new things out of nothing. They cannot create holy and righteous characters.

Their laws sound very appealing and righteous but they cannot create divine thoughts in anyone. They cannot save themselves from sin, death, and hell.

However, God's word is creative. It can put new thoughts in human beings. He can make them to think righteous thoughts like His. He can create new life, spirits, and bodies in human beings. He can create holiness, righteousness, love, joy, peace, eternity, etc. in people. His word is written in the Bible. The Bible alone can create new people.

But human laws cannot create new people out of sinners. They may look holy but they are faking it. Sooner or later, they will crush. Sin will take over their thoughts and behaviors. "Woe unto you, scribes and Pharisees, hypocrites! for ye are as graves which appear not, and the men that walk over them are not aware of them" (Luke 11:44). They will are like unmarked graves. They are unknown in heaven.

God called people who follow man-made laws hypocrites. They are faking how to be like Him. "Woe unto you, scribes and Pharisees, hypocrites! for ye make clean the outside of the cup and of the platter, but within they are full of extortion and excess. Thou blind Pharisee, cleanse first that which is within the cup and platter, that the outside of them may be clean also" (Matthew 23:25, 26).

You are a holy cup of the Lord. But He cannot drink love from you if you are hiding some sins such as living without boundaries. Do not chase the people and/or things of this world by cheating, swindling, stealing, adulterating, murdering, etc. Do not medicate yourself by excesses in food, drinks, sex, sports, etc.

They are harmful for you. Live morally and soberly before the Lord, and He will bless you. Remove those sins from your cup or soul by repentance. Ask Him to wash them away by His precious blood. He will help you. He will wash them away and make you holy. He will drink your love, faith, commitment, etc. every day. You will always be the best of friends because you are special.

Hypocrites and legalists are dead inside like white washed tombs or graves. Outside they are made to look pretty but inside, they are full of dead men and women. "Woe unto you, scribes and Pharisees, hypocrites! for ye are like unto whited sepulchres, which indeed appear beautiful outward, but are within full of dead men's bones, and of all uncleanness. Even so ye also outwardly appear righteous unto men, but within ye are full of hypocrisy and iniquity" (Matthew 23:27, 28).

Proud people may look awesome and beautiful in the exterior but inwardly they are really weak people. There is something wrong in their hearts. They are hiding dead bones and rotten flesh in their hearts.

They are full of demons. They are filled with civilian affairs but not the things of the soldiers of God. They are transgressors of the Law of God though they have put on faces of maturity, wisdom, and intelligence for the world to see.

God is very sorry for arrogant Bible scholars, Pharisees, hypocrites, and legalists. They are the kinds of the people who put the Lord's prophets to death. But how amazing it is see them pretending to be righteous! They are insulting their unbelieving ancestors as evil people when they themselves are no better.

They go to Middle East and together with the people living there; they have made the tombs of the prophets' tourist centers. They decorate them with precious stones and plant trees and flowers around them. They mourn and claim that had they lived in those times, they would never have persecuted the prophets. They are plain liars.

With the pride and arrogance of the men and women of these days, they would have been the first to pick up stones and throw at the Messiah, Moses, and the other prophets. "Woe unto you, scribes and Pharisees, hypocrites! because ye build the tombs of the prophets, and garnish the sepulchres of the righteous, And say, If we had been in the days of our fathers, we would not have been partakers with them in the blood of the prophets. Wherefore ye be witnesses unto yourselves, that ye are the children of them which killed the prophets" (Matthew 23:29–31).

There are saints living all around the people of the earth of these days. But like their faithless ancestors who persecuted the prophets, they are always looking for opportunities to destroy the saints. They claim that they are more righteousness that the truth seekers who want to live by word of God. Their actions against godly people are solid proofs that they are the descendants of murderers and God haters.

Everyone on earth was there through the people who persecuted and murdered the prophets. The whole world took part in putting the Messiah to death. Their sins killed Him.

When they murdered the Messiah, they were fulfilling up the cup of iniquity that they started to fill with in the Garden of Eden when they started to eat sin as if it is food. "Fill ye up then the measure of your fathers" (Matthew 23:32). When the world put the Messiah to death, they were filling up the cup of sin of their father, Adam.

They are acting like Satan, the master serpent. The spirits of sinners are like poisonous and deadly vipers. They are demoniacs. Unless they repent and change their behaviors, they will not escape the fires of hell. "Ye serpents, ye generation of vipers, how can ye escape the damnation of hell?" (Matthew 23:33).

It was the Messiah who was sending them holy men and women like Abel to turn them away from their sins. But they would not hear anything about God their Savior. Cain put his brother, Abel, to death for telling him the truth.

Jehoiada, the high priest, saved the family of King David from being exterminated by their grandmother, Queen Athaliah. But the Jews did not remember his kindness. They murdered his son, Zechariah in the temple for telling them to stop sinning and come back to the God of their ancestors.

Corrupt Christians are carrying on the legacy of the hypocrites of all ages. They have persecuted and/or murdered the messengers of the Lord. Prophets, disciples, counselors, teachers of the Bible, etc. have crossed and crisscrossed the earth with the Good News but no one pays attention to them.

Instead, they are persecuted and murdered. They will fight God through His followers to the end of time. "Wherefore, behold, I send unto you prophets, and wise men, and scribes: and some of them ye shall kill and crucify; and some of them shall ye scourge in your synagogues, and persecute them from city to city: That upon you may come all the righteous bloodshed upon the earth, from the blood of righteous Abel unto the blood of Zacharias son of Barachias, whom ye slew between the temple and the altar. Verily I say unto you, All these things shall come upon this generation" (Matthew

23:34–36).

They have made the churches the place of tortures just like their ancestors did in the temple. Day and night, hypocrites and legalists are persecuting and murdering the saints right in the churches. They are being chased from place to place by self-righteous Christians.

They are brands of jokes and mockeries. When the Messiah came into the world, it was no surprise that sinners put Him to death. Their hearts are filled to the full with sin.

But will sinners escape condemnation if they persist in their sins? They will not escape being condemned to be executed by hell fires if they continue to slave for Satan. They will pay for the blood of the Messiah that they shed on Mount Calvary.

All sinners are representing in the one City that loved to shed the blood of the prophets and of the Messiah. She is Jerusalem. How long will God continue to weep over self-righteous Jerusalem? "O Jerusalem, Jerusalem, thou that killest the prophets, and stonest them which are sent unto thee, how often would I have gathered thy children together, even as a hen gathereth her chickens under her wings, and ye would not! Behold, your house is left unto you desolate" (Matthew 23:37, 38).

Jerusalem was the murder of prophets and of the Messiah. She stoned some of them to death. She crucified others. How many times has God tried to gather her in His arms like a chicken that gathers her pullets under her wings when an eagle is encircling them overhead!

He is willing to save her and all sinners even today. She represents all the sinners of the earth who love to murder holy people including the Messiah. But no one wants the protection of God. They all think that they are the All-Powerful God and can, therefore, save themselves from sin, sorrows, demons, death, and hell. But there will come a time when their strength will give you. They will neither be able to solve their individual problems nor the problems of the whole world.

They will turn their attention to the Messiah. "For I say unto you, Ye shall not see me henceforth, till ye shall say, Blessed is he that cometh in the name of the Lord" (Matthew 23:39).

2. God made people for relationships

Out of one man, even Adam, has God created people are many as the dust of the earth or the stars in the sky. All the nations of the earth came from one mother called Eve. Adam and Eve were mere vessels to produce children for Him. He is the true Father and Mother of the children who lives on this earth.

He had planned the parents of each child and where he or she should live long before He made heaven and earth. He decreed that everyone should live eternally in peace, joy, love, etc. Each child was to have a great successful life. He or she would share His divine life. But demons and sins tried to ruin His plans for His beautiful children. Still, He is down here and fighting for them.

He has given them the privilege to place orders on His table as to what they need. Because He is their God, He will fulfill all their needs. But the best thing He wants them to do is to long for Him with a yearning that is deeper than words. If they can place Him above their very own lives as the most important, loving, and loveliest Person on earth, He will not delay to save them from all their sins.

They will not only find Him but touch Him. There is no one who lives on this earth that is too sinful to be saved. He is ready to save anyone who calls on His holy and powerful name. "And hath made of one blood all nations of men for to dwell on all the face of the earth, and hath determined the times before appointed, and the bounds of their habitation;

That they should seek the Lord, if haply they might feel after him, and find him, though he be not far from every one of us: For in him we live, and move, and have our being; as certain also of your own poets have said, For we are also his offspring" (Acts 17:26–28).

If the people of the earth can breathe through Him, they can also be saved by Him. He has given them brains to think, mouths to talk, limbs for movements, etc. But He does not want them to be short-lived. He wants to glorify them with His own tremendous and earth-shaking glories. He wants to change their mortalities into immortalities.

Let them listen to their wise men and women and especially the Bible. They will know beyond any possible doubt that He fathered them. They grew out of His All-Powerful creative Spirit.

God made men and women so that they can have relationships. You cannot fake it. It is a relationship between a sweet and lovely Daddy and His adorable children. The one and only true God who made heaven and earth as His work implements for producing greater glories for Himself is not one of you or anyone of the vessels He has made for His work.

He is not one of the dishes He created to display His glory such as an angel, man, woman, sun, moon, star, etc. He does not live in a dish such as the earth but outside her. He is infinite and greater in power than mere dishes, vessels or work implements.

The inventor or manufacturer is never the invention. He or she is the brain behind the invention. He or she is more intelligent and power than what he or she invents or manufactures.

The Creator is All-Benevolent or All-Loving. He is Love within Himself. Loving angels and people does not improve His character and make Him a better Person. The Cross shows that He is love but it does not make improvements on His love as it would have done had an angel or human being died for the sins of the world. He is eternally All-Loving whether His children love Him or not and will remain so forever. "But God, who is rich in mercy, for his great love wherewith he loved us, Even when we were dead in sins, hath quickened us together with Christ, (by grace ye are saved;)

And hath raised us up together, and made us sit together in heavenly places in Christ Jesus: That in the ages to come he might shew the exceeding riches of his grace in his kindness toward us through Christ Jesus" (Ephesians 2:4-7).

He is a very rich and wealthy Person in love and mercy to all. The beauty of His love shines most brightly on the Cross. His love for you grows intensely strong and multiplied infinitely from everlasting to everlasting. You are already dead in sin before you were born. So His love had to receive you into His arms on the day you were born because of the Cross. Otherwise, no one could have lived had He not resurrected from the Cross and gave pardon and life to the earth to continue to exist.

You have died with Christ on the Cross of Calvary. You have risen with Him from the dead on the third day. You are sitting with Him on the throne of everlasting powers in the third heaven ruling countless junior heavens and worlds that are swirling round and round below His feet.

Since the Lord has now surrounded you with the good fortunes of super grace that comes only from a divine heart like His and everlasting life that comes only from Him. Seize His gentlest and most caring love without delay and step into the next world. She is blissful, peaceful, lovely and eternal.

Sinners have no an all-benevolent or unconditional love to be able to forgive themselves and others. One of them was Cain. He preached lies when he claimed that fruits can save people from their sins and create in them eternal life. "And in process of time it came to pass, that Cain brought of the fruit of the ground an offering unto the LORD.

And Abel, he also brought of the firstlings of his flock and of the fat thereof. And the LORD had respect unto Abel and to his offering: But unto Cain and to his offering he had not respect. And Cain was very wroth, and his countenance fell" (Genesis 4:3–5). Nothing else spiritual arrogance led to the downfall of the person who first opened the womb of a woman. You will fall too if you create your own way of reaching heaven.

You, as a mere vessel or dish into which He poured His Spirit, cannot think that you can be God the Creator. You cannot create yourself or anything. Whatever you may do for God such as building for Him churches, schools, hospitals, preaching, healing, etc. goes as far as a dish is able to perform the work assigned to it by its manufacturer.

You cannot assume the powers of divinity and think that you can create God or gods. "God that made the world and all things therein, seeing that he is Lord of heaven and earth, dwelleth not in temples made with hands; Neither is worshipped with men's hands, as though he needed anything, seeing he giveth to all life, and breath, and all things" (Acts 17:24, 25). Mere men and women cannot mold God with their hands and give Him body, flesh or spirit in the form of images.

His brains are not wired to crave food, water, attention, love, etc. like they do. He does not receive His satisfactions and fulfillments from inferior creatures but from His own Spirit. He is satisfied with who He is and what He is doing.

He is already supplying His own life to multitudes of beings in heaven, on the earth and in all the inhabitable stars all over the endless universes. He helps them to breathe moment by moment in order to keep them alive. He does that not only to His children but all the pets such as the animals He has created to keep them company.

He always hears the prayers of those who are humble at heart. "He will regard the prayer of the destitute, and not despise their prayer" (Psalms 102:17).

He has opened door wide open for your prayers to enter into His heart. He prepared the way for your prayers to reach His heart. It is the most excellent you will appreciate. It is the way of love.

The way is wide open for you. And the best loves of all is the Cross. It is God's own life sacrificed for your life.

He has never refused to comfort you in your sorrows. He does not turn His back on you when you fall into sin. He is right there beside you. He has forgiven you all your sins.

All that He wants to do is to help find true life. "For he hath not despised nor abhorred the affliction of the afflicted; neither hath he hid his face from him; but when he cried unto him, he heard" (Psalms 22:24).

He has not made you of a nonentity to Himself. He has not shaken you out of life. He has neither denied the right to exist as one of the human beings on earth nor access to Him in order to be saved. He does not hate sinners. He does not turn a blind eye to their suffering.

He heard your prayers for help long before you were born. He knows all about your needs. He knows that you need His help before you asked for it. He knows all about the prayers you would pray in your life time before He created the heavens and the earth. He is the Answer to all your needs.

He listens very attentively when you are praying. He
keeps your requests in His heart for all times to come. He is
ready to shoulder all your problems. You are worth as much as
His own life.

Please love, praise and adore Him as long as there is
breath in your soul. Whether you have lived a fairly good life
or receive hard knocks all your life, just love and worship
Him, anyway. "Jesus said unto him, Thou shalt love the Lord
thy God with all thy heart, and with all thy soul, and with all
thy mind" (Matthew 22:37).

He has never humiliated, shamed or tried to murder you.
He loves you and sacrificed His own Son to keep this world
alive to give you chance to repent and be saved. He is praying
that you may come to your sense and repent from all your sins
during this probationary period. His blood will wash away
your sins, and you will be saved.

His heart is filled with tender, sweet, and fiery love that
sets things in motion in heaven and on the earth to bless your
life. He went to the deepest place in hell and defied death in
order to save. He chose risks in order to give you stability and
peace.

He might not have risen from the dead had He sinned. But
He took the leap of faith and died for your sake. Thanks be to
God! He rose from the dead and so will you. He will do great
things for you.

He will calm the storms in your life. He will bring you
safe home to heaven. "With him is wisdom and strength, he
hath counsel and understanding. With him is strength and
wisdom: the deceived and the deceiver are his" (Job 12: 13,
16).

He is All-Wise. He is All-Powerful. He is your Counselor.
He will guide you throughout your life. Everyone who
worships himself or herself is blinded by his or her pride. He
or she depends on Him alone for life. Even Satan has no
inherent life in himself. He depends on God every second of
his life to keep alive.

Hold onto God for truth and righteousness. He is the
Tutor of all the wise men and women of this earth. He gives
them very loving, compassionate, and understanding hearts.
He will enlighten your mind until you, too, have an

understanding and wise heart. You will be wise and intelligent. "He discovereth deep things out of darkness, and bringeth out to light the shadow of death" (Job 12:22).

He will heal you even though you are living in this world that is filled with the deep darkness of sin. He is watching over you. He will make life meaningful to you. He will save you from this living death. He will resurrect you from the grave. You will live in the land of sunshine of love, joy, peace, eternity, etc.

Indeed, He is your New Jerusalem. He is the city of pure delight. He is your Mother. "Rejoice ye with Jerusalem, and be glad with her, all ye that love her: rejoice for joy with her, all ye that mourn for her: That ye may suck, and be satisfied with the breasts of her consolations; that ye may milk out, and be delighted with the abundance of her glory" (Isaiah 66:10, 11).

He may look down and out today but hold onto Him. He is going to win the last battle. You are going to see peace in this world. You will join the other saints in celebrating the dawn of the new universes and the earth. You will dance and shake your bones lose because of the tremendous joy that will fill your heart. You are the people that He loves very much. He will give you everlasting peace.

You will celebrate the arrival of the New City of Jerusalem all of you people who have longed for a city that has no sin, death, criminals, coups, wars, etc. You have prayed, mourned, and wept all your lives for a city of peace, and you will get her.

You will suck God's breaths that flow with milk that is sweeter than honey. His large cool hand will cover you like a tent and shield you from farther troubles. He will stroke your head and comfort you like a mother comforting a baby feeding on her breasts.

He will dry your tears. You will forget all the hurts and humiliations you received in this world, and how they ruined your life. He will give you all the comfort that you need. Your provisions will flow like boundlessly and endlessly like milk from a mother's breasts that will nourish a baby with good health.

You will own all the abundance of the new heaven and

universes. You will be happy and satisfied with the provisions the Lord will supply for you. They will enhance your powerful prestige before the eyes of the inhabitants of other stars. You will be well-provided and will not ask any help from them.

Peace is flowing from heaven as deep and wide as the oceans. "For thus saith the LORD, Behold, I will extend peace to her like a river, and the glory of the Gentiles like a flowing stream: then shall ye suck, ye shall be borne upon her sides, and be dandled upon her knees" (Isaiah 66:12).

The converted Jews and Gentiles will join forces and form one nation of peace and goodwill towards each other. They will all sit down at the breasts of their Creator and suckle life eternal. He will play with them, tickle, and tease them. He will carry them in His arms wherever He goes. He will never put them down or abandon them.

His nutritious milk will nourish them back to health that is eternal. "And when ye see this, your heart shall rejoice, and your bones shall flourish like an herb: and the hand of the LORD shall be known toward his servants, and his indignation toward his enemies" (Isaiah 66:14).

Their bones will be young and strong. They will be full of youthful vitality like the green medical herbs in the garden. Their hearts will almost burst with deep and inexpressible joy in seeing how health and eternally youthful they are.

They will know for sure that it was none other but the All-Wise God who has given them this good health. Because of all the good things He will do for them, they will vow to serve Him as His slaves forever. And to make them eternal happy and safe, He will eliminate all enemies and obstacles that will threaten to destroy their good health.

References:

Chapter 1

1.   Flavius Josephus, Antiquities of the Jews – Book
     XVIII, From the Banishment of
     Archelaus to the Departure of the Jews
     from Babylon, # 1.

   Chapter 3

2.   <u>Flavius Josephus, Antiquities of the Jews – Book
     XVIII</u>, From the Banishment of
     Archelaus to the Departure of the Jews
     from Babylon, # 1.

3.   Wikipedia: Annas.

Made in the USA
Las Vegas, NV
16 August 2023

76195306R00066